# A Life Complete

*Emotional and Spiritual Growth*
*for Midlife and Beyond*

# Sallirae Henderson

SCRIBNER

New York   London   Toronto   Sydney   Singapore

SCRIBNER
1230 Avenue of the Americas
New York, NY 10020

SCRIBNER and design are trademarks of Macmillan Library Reference USA, Inc.,
used under license by Simon & Schuster, the publisher of this work.

Designed by Brooke Koven
Set in Dante

Manufactured in the United States of America

1    3    5    7    9    10    8    6    4    2

Library of Congress Cataloging-in-Publication Data
Henderson, Sallirae, date.
A life complete / Sallirae Henderson.
p. cm.
Includes bibliographical references and index.
1. Middle aged persons—Psychology. 2. Middle aged persons—Psychological aspects.
3. Aged—Psychology. 4. Aging—Psychological aspects. 5. Spiritual life. I. Title.
BF724.6 .H46 2000
155.6'7—dc21        00-025336

ISBN 0-684-83775-7

To the residents and staff of Willamette View, Inc.,
Portland, Oregon

and to my wonderful sons,
who are almost as old as I am:
Neal Hoff Melton
Tyler "Ty" Melton

and to the one who holds my heart steady,
Joseph Anthony Coglianese

# Contents

# A Life
# Complete

# Introduction

The birth of this material took place at the end of life, unfolding itself as I counseled elders in their last years. Each person's sharing of experience opened a window to the decades he or she had lived before. Standing at the end of these long lives, I was intimately involved with the final consequences of their early choices and learned more about living than I'd ever thought possible. Beginning with the internal strengths of elders who were coping well, I backtracked into their early decisions about life, their values, beliefs, philosophy, and theology. On the flip side, exploring the history of elders who were unable to cope with old age revealed early choices and attitudes that had resulted in unresolved despair, rage, and general misery.

Stepping back for a wider view, I looked at these elders' experiences in the context of our culture and gained new insight into how deeply our society's values and negative attitudes toward aging impact the quality of our lives. As the moon's gravitational pull determines the earth's tides, so do the values and expectations of society pull on our potential for individual choice, often blinding us to our options altogether. It became alarmingly clear to me that what I choose now in middle age will have a direct bearing on the emotional and spiritual quality of my last years, and that these same choices are foundational to my current experience and whether I will die a completed human being or an unfinished one.

Alerted to the long-term consequences of my current beliefs and actions, I began paying closer attention to them. Now I could see where I was putting important things off, risking compromising my values, not paying attention to what was true for me and to what I needed to stay healthy emotionally, spiritually, and physically. I began examining my values, asking if they were relevant to the whole of my life or only the immediate, culturally defined issues before me. And with no small amount of grief, I finally reconciled myself to the reality that the only permanent fact of life is that nothing is permanent.

Twenty years ago, as a hospital and hospice chaplain, I began working with dying people. Most of the patients I saw were young to middle-aged adults with a terminal illness. Later I worked with elders, first as the pastor of a church and then as a full-time counselor to the six hundred residents of a continuing-care retirement community. Dying young and dying old are different. Young and middle-aged adults are still creating who they are. Knowing that this process is being cut short, many take stock of their lives, facing who they have been and what they will never be. Their self-exploration can, and frequently does, bring about startling transformation in their final weeks or months. But this kind of life examination is not so easy for a person who has done things the same way for fifty, sixty, or seventy years of adulthood. When we are old, we are more ourselves than we have ever been before; over the

decades our personalities and habits of thinking have solidified. After so many years of reinforcing familiar patterns of
behavior and thinking, most people simply don't know how to
perceive things any other way. Or, to admit they have lived for
so long mistaking the superficial for reality is to face the fact
too late that life could have been more satisfying and meaningful. For most, such a realization would be too devastating
to bear.

This book describes the basic emotional and spiritual skills
that are necessary to ensure continued growth and meaning
into our last years, even if we are ill and disabled. These tools
are what it will take to attain what I have named "completion
of self" before we die. It is necessary to begin considering
these skills early because it can take decades for them to grow
and develop into the best fit for your unique experience and
personality.

Looking at your current life from the perspective of the
end of it may feel to you like having a bucket of cold water
thrown onto your psyche—that's how it felt to me in the
beginning. But now that I have lived with these concepts for
several years, I have experienced a relaxing into my life, seeing and appreciating its shapes, dimensions, and colors. I am
in an ongoing process of discarding beliefs and values that
can't reach deeper than the surface, while at the same time
my core values are expanding, becoming stronger and more
carefully defined as I consciously test them. I spend less time
living by default and more time conscious of the beauty and
pain and love both within me and in the world. Living with
the knowledge of the end, I sense, more than ever before, a
purpose for my living. I have become—and am becoming—
more truly and authentically alive.

Throughout this book I will use the last years of our lives

as a reference point and goal to guide us in the present. When I refer to these last years or the last stage of life, what I'm *not* talking about are those golden years following retirement when you and your spouse and friends travel all over the world, attend exciting Elderhostel programs, play tennis every day, and take up skydiving. The stage from which I derived these concepts comes some time later. I'm talking about the years after you've had to give up your car because slow reflexes have made you a menace on the road; the years after your spouse has died or has gone into a nursing home; the years when your busy family members may be lovingly attentive but you worry that your needs are preventing them from living their own lives. Your energy and stamina levels may be so low that getting out of bed, getting dressed, and preparing two meals a day exhaust most of your physical resources. Many or all of your longtime friends have already died and your best friend is in a nursing home across town; she has had a stroke and cannot speak, so you have no way to be together, even by telephone. Poor vision limits your reading to twenty minutes, and the print has to be large; or hearing loss makes it difficult to follow conversation, which causes you to respond inappropriately at times. A less efficient digestive system has forced you to give up your favorite spicy foods—and chocolate. Palsy or arthritis, or both, prevent you from the needlework, gardening, woodworking, or writing that calmed and nurtured you in the past. Now, even cold sober, you're unsteady on your feet so you can hardly risk the glass of wine you used to enjoy every evening.

In spite of these limitations, your major organs—those miraculous components that keep the body operating for so many years—continue to work more or less faithfully. They may function well enough to keep you alive for another decade or more, perhaps with enough energy to care for yourself at home. Or your limitations may make it necessary to hire in-home health aides or to move to a nursing home or other institutional care setting.

Having cured most of the illnesses that used to kill us, medical science can take credit for buying us better health and additional decades of living. These new years are a new stage added onto our life span. But the same medical victories that have prolonged our lives have also preserved us to live into those years most associated with chronic disability and illness. In past generations, only the very healthy lived into their eighties and nineties; now most of us will, healthy or not.

Around the time I began organizing this book, I received a postcard from a ninety-seven-year-old gentleman touring obscure corners of China. Two years earlier he'd had his ninety-fifth birthday picture taken while he was standing at the North Pole. Back at the retirement community, I saw a couple in their eighties playing tennis every day. By the time I arrived at work in the morning a group of women in their seventies and eighties were already out walking their daily two and a half miles, and another woman was just leaving for her daily Jazzercise class. I would see her later in the day dressed in high heels and a business suit, looking fashionably smart and twenty-five years younger than her age, which was eighty-six.

Frankly, I was annoyed by all this vim and vigor. These exceptional people had become the standard for "how things ought to be" for everyone. Disabled and ill elders used these examples as proof of their own failure. I spent an inordinate amount of time undergirding the plummeting self-esteem of those who held themselves to a standard that was personally impossible for them to achieve.

Our entire life span is made up of challenging tasks that

can bring frustration at every turn. But they can also bring—
if we're open to them—new insight, understanding, and a
glimpse of possibilities we were unable to see before. I have
seen this same process of discovery alive and vital, both in
healthy and in sick and disabled elders, right up to the time of
their death. Like the previous stages of our lives, this last one
has its own territories to explore and to learn from. Finding
meaning in late life, especially if we are afflicted with chronic
illness or disability, can be difficult, intricate, and tedious
work, but it consists of the details that complete the structure
of our lives. This productivity takes place on the level of the
heart and the mind. Like constructing a home, building the
infrastructure of our lives and applying the finishing touches
can take a long time. But when it is done, if the work and
material are of good quality, we get to experience the exquis-
ite satisfaction of knowing it is complete and sound.

The word "completion," as I use it in this work, is not the
same as being "finished." I bought a 5,000-piece jigsaw puzzle
a few years ago and set it up in my living room. Four months
later the joined and unjoined pieces had gathered so much
dust that I couldn't stand feeling the grit on them. I'd also
become tired of the project and discouraged by its difficulty. I
boxed it up and gave it to a friend whose teenaged son put it
together in a couple of weeks. I had finished with it—was sick
of it, in fact; it was my friend's son who completed it. This is
what I mean by the difference between being finished and
being completed. Many elders I have worked with have
declared themselves "finished," meaning that they were sick
and tired of being sick and tired and dependent on others.
They wanted to die, the sooner the better. This state of mind
is usually accompanied by depression, passivity, anger, and
withdrawal. An elder's statement that he is "finished" may

mean that he feels complete, but more often it means that he feels depressed and hopeless.

I want to come to my final stage and say that the project that has been my life is complete—that I am a completed human being, or more specifically a completed Sallirae. I've lived long enough to know that the process of creating and working through one's life includes discomfort and often heartbreaking emotional and spiritual work. There are facts of my life that I would just as soon not stir up or even remember, things about myself that I don't want to acknowledge, both good and bad. But the integration of even these uncomfortable realities is important to arriving at completion before I die.

It does not help that we have few—if any—media role models for being old and disabled. Our contemporary culture does not offer us a framework of meaning or any teaching or guidelines for this last stage of life. Because of the lack of personal preparation and respectful acknowledgment from our society, most people currently enter this stage of life without the skills, support, or hope from which they can derive strength and nurture. It's no wonder many of us who are younger spend so much time and money trying to prevent ourselves from becoming old—or, as one cosmetics commercial puts it (using a model who must be at least thirty-two), "I don't mind growing old, I just don't want to look old!"

If we have bought into our society's myth of eternal youth, we will come to our last years in a state of arrested development. The pressure to remain forever young prevents us from allowing the natural changes of age to shape us into our elder selves. We cannot, under these circumstances, adjust to the reality of being old, especially if we are ill and in need of assistance.

Our last years of declining stamina and failing physical systems are a process of stripping away the nonessential. We learn, frequently with great pain, that the roles, status, abilities, and activities that we thought we could never do without have in fact become irrelevant. What we are left with is the heart of the person we have become. For some, that will be life's blessing; for others, it will be a curse.

In our busy lives it's easy *not* to be aware that the choices we make today could have long-lasting and ultimately devastating consequences. Take the example of Elizabeth, a woman in her late eighties who, still living independently in her own home, was deeply miserable. Her face tight with tension, she described herself as a lifelong good Christian. But she had never been happy. Her reactions to people and events had always been a litany of judgment and criticism. She told me that she should never have married the man she had been with for over sixty years; she could hardly stand to be in the same room with him and secretly hoped he would die soon. Her grown children struggled to love her, but to preserve their own sanity they made their visits infrequent and short. Whatever the original source of her unhappiness, Elizabeth had built her entire life on it. Never satisfied and always critical, she alienated everyone around her. Another example is Ethel and Bill, who in their fifty-six years of marriage had habitually chosen the safety of appearances and acquisition over a deeper engagement with life and each other. Bill spent the last months of his life in a nursing home watching television, occasionally making references to getting better and going home. Ethel fluttered nervously about his bed, trying to engage him in small talk about the weather, their neighbors, and the TV programs she had seen. The gulf between them was highlighted by his lack of response to her.

Bill died watching a TV game show. He and his wife had never spoken of their shared lives, or of their appreciation for each other. They had never said goodbye. It was as if all those years together meant nothing, had never even happened.

When we don't acknowledge the finish line, we have no cues for which direction we should take today. By the time we finally approach the end of the race, we will be so lost and disoriented that we'll be in danger of collapsing without ever reaching the goal. In avoiding the knowledge of our eventual decline and death we are not equipping ourselves for the difficult demands those final miles will make on us, and we may find out too late that we were never truly alive. If, on the other hand, we accept the fact of our mortality and integrate that knowledge into our current consciousness, we will be able to move closer to the essence of who we are. This is where we can discover larger meanings. This knowing will be our most powerful internal resource as we live out our lives. Consciously allowing ourselves to be honed and deepened by experience—including loss and dependence—we can attain the emotional and spiritual depth that is wisdom, plus an internal freedom that engages fully with life even as we are dying. These will be the crowning achievements of a long and completed life. Late life, even with chronic illness, carries the potential for depth of meaning and purpose not possible at earlier stages.

It's not my intention to create a new standard for how we "should" live our last years. No matter how well prepared, how mature, or how wise we are, becoming old and ill will throw us into some hard places emotionally and spiritually. We will grieve, and our self-esteem may take some shattering blows. Even our hope may be crushed at times. This doesn't mean we've become weak in character or didn't do our preparations "right." The disappointments have more to do with the fact that these last years involve our whole selves more than any other stage of adulthood, and we'll have very few avenues of escape from that reality.

I asked an elder what, if anything, she has gained in her last years. She replied that she has become quiet. "It's an inside feeling," she explained. "I have nothing to prove, and that is a wonderful feeling. It doesn't mean that I am cutting myself off from the goings-on in the world." She regularly writes letters to columnists and politicians, sharing with them what she has learned in her eighty-four years. Her stamina and energy are seriously compromised by her congested and failing heart, but even so there is a sense of well-being and resilient strength about her. "I feel settled within myself," she says. "I am at peace."

Knowing that the end is moving ever closer to each of us, seeing how much energy and talent we squander on what is only temporary, I felt—and feel—a compelling need to share what I've learned. We are already planting the seeds of our last years of life. Whatever seeds we sow today will be the harvest we live with when we are too old to rework the fields.

# PART I

# Emotional Preparation

The first three chapters of Part 1 explore the three emotional attributes and skills that I've observed as being basic to clarity and well-being as we mature. If you use these concepts as a foundation for growth, your understanding, experience, and being will branch outward in directions you did not foresee and upward to heights you did not expect. At the same time, you will put down roots from which to receive the emotional and spiritual nutrients you need to gain and maintain a resilient strength. The fourth chapter, on Alzheimer's disease, is a departure from the rest of the book. I was motivated to include it by a 1996 survey taken in the United States asking people what they feared about growing old. Fear of having Alzheimer's was second only to being in a nursing home, so I included this chapter to broaden our perception of this disease and hopefully to allay some of the fears surrounding it.

Although emotional and spiritual growth can and often do intertwine, I have treated them separately—emotional growth in Part I, spiritual growth in Part II—both for ease of discussion and because they function differently in the psyche. Emotional feelings and behavior begin and reside within the individual even though they are often—and appropriately—a reaction to something that occurs outside of us. Spirituality also occurs within the individual, of course, but differs in that it is a relationship with a thing or idea that is experienced as larger than oneself and that gives life meaning.

Emotional clarity—knowledge of oneself—is absolutely necessary if we are to grow into a spirituality that is not distorted by unexamined motives for power, status, or escape from the uncomfortable details of everyday life. Spirituality is not a shortcut to happiness, because no matter how devout we may be, we will always carry with us the baggage of any unresolved psychological issues. People who operate from a spirituality contaminated by these unresolved issues tend to claim superiority and in their actions seem to have missed the point of the teachings they've chosen to follow. Through word and action, no matter how good their intentions may be, they can and do damage others emotionally, spiritually, and even physically.

I have met many elders who have cloaked themselves in religious or New Age thought to cover up those parts of themselves they cannot, or will not, accept. They do not have an easy time in their last years. Their unfinished emotional issues seep through the religious veneer that can no longer hide and protect them. They feel lost and abandoned: their spirituality, after all, can grow no deeper than they are willing to go within themselves. Some sink into long-term despair; others grow so bitter and judgmental that their care providers, including their families, spend as little time with them as possible. It's a devastating discovery to find in late life that one has orphaned oneself for a belief system by which one has lived superficially.

The purpose of the concepts in Part I is, first and foremost, to bring you back to yourself—to learn who you truly are and what you really need. Having this self-knowledge, you can function as a whole human being, engaged in life with integrity, love, and satisfaction spiced by moments of pure joy. If you hold the ideas in the next three chapters as reference points for your growth and maturing, you will reach old age with few regrets, having lived a more fulfilled and satisfying life.

# I

# Befriending Yourself

Eighty-four-year-old Lucille phoned my office and asked me to come see her. When I went to her apartment we sat in silence for a long time. I asked how she was doing. "Fine," she answered flatly. More silence. Finally she noted the weather: "Cold today." Again, silence. I waited, curbing my urge to initiate conversation so as to leave the door open for her statement. None came. I still didn't know why she had asked to see me. Finally, with soft, sparse words, I began to gently explore her silence, looking for the reason she had felt the need to see me. During the following weeks of my visiting her, the problem gradually emerged. A well-educated woman and accomplished musician, Lucille had lived her life by her intellect, ignoring her emotions. Widowed fifteen years earlier, she spent sleepless nights alone in bed with a person she didn't know—herself. She had no experience or language for knowing what she needed, much less what she wanted. She was a shell of mute despair.

Treating ourselves as a best friend is an important factor in the quality of our current living and will be crucial in our last years. It's the only way we can gain an intimate and supportive knowledge of who we are and what we need. Being familiar with—and able to articulate—our wants and needs gives us some control of our lives, and is absolutely essential when we are old and may have to rely on others to do what we can no longer do for ourselves.

To know ourselves in a way that is supportive, we must become our own friend. This doesn't mean we don't need other people, but it does mean that we can't afford to be totally reliant on someone else to be the "expert" on us. Many people rely on their lover, spouse, family members, and roles to define their identity and worth. When the defining persons or roles are gone, the survivors may be left with no sense of self and severe limitations in their ability to advocate for themselves. This lack of knowledge and skill contributes to long-term depression and illness; for some elders it can even hasten death.

When I think of what it means to be my own friend, I look to the friends I already have. They fall into concentric circles, like the ripples that would encircle me if I were to drop into the center of a pond. These circles are occupied by people who have various degrees of impact on my life. Generally, acquaintances and some co-workers, connected to my life in important but peripheral ways, are in the circle farthest out. The next circle in is occupied by professional colleagues and people whose services I depend on and whom I also like and enjoy. I relate to the people in both outer circles on the level of small talk, humor, and business matters. The next circle toward me is a group of friends whose knowledge of each other runs deeper than the small talk of parties and professions. The circle closest to me, the smallest one, is occupied by people I refer to as best friends. This group can be made up of several people or one person. These friends care about my well being and are likely to show up or phone when I'm sick. We can spend several hours over dinner talking about what's important to us and we tell each other things about ourselves that we wouldn't share with many other people. Through their acceptance and affection, they reflect back to me my value as a human being. We keep each other company when life becomes tedious, frightening, or overwhelming.

The most important thing a best friend does is accept and trust us. When I'm in an emotional funk these friends will listen without belittling my feelings or trying to distract me with advice. They hear my experience and express their regret for my suffering, helping me feel less alone. They are genuinely happy when I've achieved something that's important to me. With these friends I can express even the dark secrets of my heart because I know they will keep them confidential and not judge me for the issues they know I struggle with. I feel safe with them, because I know they will not use what I tell them to hurt or manipulate me. This safety is created by mutual respect, affection, forgiveness, acceptance, and trust. Befriending ourselves requires the same kind of investment—the development of kindness, trust, forgiveness, and affection toward ourselves.

Becoming our own friend also includes looking into the darkest corners of our minds and hearts and acknowledging what is there. I can assure you that for those of us who work in mental health—including our own—the mind and heart offer no surprises: jealousy, greed, destructive ambition, hatred, lust, self-righteousness, and fear lurk in all of us to some degree at some time. Admitting them into our consciousness may cause us discomfort, even shame, but if we don't acknowledge these parts that we cannot like, they will stay hidden. Shut off from help and healing, they will emerge quietly and drive our behaviors in ways we don't understand and may not like. It's crucial for us not to unconsciously live our lives from these dark places, only to be left with their emotional consequences in our last years.

Eighty-six-year-old Valerie is an example of someone who never looked at the deeper parts of herself that she would probably not have liked. A few minutes after phoning me for an appointment, Valerie pushed her walker through the door of my office and sat down on one of the two wing-back chairs. I came out from behind my desk and joined her in the other chair, wondering why on earth she had asked to see me. Valerie barely topped five feet in her two-inch heels. She wore stylish, expensive clothes and would have been quite attractive were it not for the perpetual scowl on her face, which left the impression that no one ever quite lived up to her expectations. Unfortunately, it wasn't a misleading facade—she was perennially critical. I was astonished that she had sought me out for any kind of counsel.

Years earlier, when she had applied from another state for residence at the retirement facility, her adult daughter, who lived near the community, contacted the facility's administration and asked them not to accept her mother's application. Relating to her mother was so intolerable that years earlier she had moved out of the state in which her mother lived, hoping to gain some distance from their toxic relationship. After Valerie moved in (the facility had no legal grounds for rejecting her application), mother and daughter rarely saw each other. The few meetings they did have ended with anger on both sides because Valerie never failed to point out her daughter's shortcomings.

When Valerie came to my office that day, she had recently

recovered from a serious illness and had been discharged from the nursing home to return to her own apartment. The illness had been a foretaste of her mortality, and she was shaken by the knowledge of it. She had come to ask me how she could make sure her daughter would inherit the most possible money from her estate. I referred her to people qualified to deal with financial issues, and then we talked about her recent illness. What stood out in my mind was the frantic tone of her original question about maximum inheritance for her daughter. At some level she realized that this was the only way she had left to love and care for her child, a love her daughter would not receive until after Valerie's death.

If we cannot face the truth of ourselves and our actions, we, like Valerie, will never discover the value inherent in our own and other's lives. We will be blinded to opportunities for love and satisfaction. Unexamined motives that cause us to behave in puzzling or offensive ways will drive people away, as Valerie drove her daughter and others away. Like Valerie and Lucille, the woman at the beginning of this chapter, we will remain a stranger to ourselves and to others. As these two women's last years demonstrated, disappointments that we don't grieve or own up to can cause us to become depressed, bitter, critical of others, and physically ill. Likewise, if we don't recognize our wish for power, control, or recognition, we can seriously hurt the people around us by using them, pushing them aside, or belittling their efforts so that we can hold the more powerful position. The unlovely parts of ourselves are hard to admit to, even harder to let go of. But they extract a high price from the quality of our daily lives and can leave us alone and bereft in our last years. They are simply not worth it. By never admitting we've made errors in judgment or that our motives are often self-serving—in other words, by remaining estranged from parts of ourselves—we can never develop self-trust, self-respect, or honesty with ourselves or another person. This ignorance creates huge gulfs both within us and between us and those who might otherwise give us their respect and affection. Unable to trust ourselves, we feel even more out of control.

If you have a history of trauma or abuse, I caution you not to explore your darkness alone but to engage the services of a compassionate mental health professional with special training in these areas. Reliving trauma or an abusive history can retraumatize you, making you feel even worse. A good therapist will know how to control the exploration and keep you safe emotionally so that you are not overwhelmed and retraumatized.

Perhaps you find yourself without close friends. If so, just take note of that fact without judging yourself. There's probably a very good reason why you've had the need to hold people at a distance. If you feel you would like to change this, it's time for some soul-searching, including taking a look at your history. You might also consider having the assistance of a psychotherapist. A good one can help his or her clients see the forest from the trees, usually much faster than the clients could on their own.

Our discomfort with what lives inside us is one reason why so much of our thinking is oriented to the future rather than the present moment—this moment—which contains *all* of who we are, our strengths and satisfactions as well as our cowardice and greed. It's easy to stay busy working or planning projects, distracting ourselves to keep from being present in the here and now. Otherwise we might have to feel all that is both good and unpleasant about our lives. Like Lucille and Valerie, our inattention keeps us from experiencing the openness of heart and mind that would allow us to see the small nurturing intimacies that life offers us every day—the love and need of our child; the respect reflected to us in someone's eyes; the greeting smile of a stranger; a tiny sparrow perched on the tallest tip of a tree. These small events, if we can take them in and treasure them, have a cumulative effect—the more attentive we are to them, the more there are to see. In hard times, times of "roughing" it emotionally or spiritually, we can often keep going on the memory of these warm moments, sights, and sounds.

Our need for constant activity and distraction to avoid the full knowledge of what lives inside us dovetails nicely with the consumerism that our society pushes us toward. I've spent many hours inside a windowless mall shopping for warm-weather clothing on some of the most beautiful days of the year. By the time I come out of the mall, the sun is going down and clouds on the horizon are signaling the end of the warm weather for a while. And there have been occasions when I've looked forward to quiet evenings at home and have stopped after work to shop for all possible food and comfort contingencies, only to find, when I finally arrive home, that it's time to go to bed. This is time I've unthinkingly spent preparing for life rather than living it. Distracting behaviors of this kind keep us from experiencing our real needs. I expect that on my deathbed I'll wish I had spent those beautiful days outside, no matter what I wore, and that I'd spent more quiet evenings at home relaxing, with or without the pizza and cookies. I may also wish I had noticed earlier that I'd never gotten around to visiting Morocco and that I'd been too busy with other interests to be the mother my children deserved.

These revelations can be devastating when it's too late to do anything about them. It's the avoidance of our inner truth that causes us not to notice how we are spending our time. Self-ignorance prevents us from realizing that we haven't yet developed priorities that support our wholeness, that we are living life by default. Realizing this in old age, when it's too late to do anything about it, can drop one into a bottomless pit of despair.

The psychoanalyst Alice Miller has written several books about how we are taught from childhood not to listen to our own truths but to conform instead to needs and rules imposed by outside forces.[1] Since this has been the case for most of us, learning to listen to our inner voice, which will tell us our personal truth, can require considerable intent and discipline. In an effort to teach this skill, one psychiatrist has his patients wear a watch with an alarm set to go off five times a day. Each time the alarm sounds, the wearers are supposed to stop whatever they are doing for five minutes and write down how they are feeling in mind, body, and spirit. For many of us, this kind of regimen is what it takes to find out how we are and what we need to support our mental, spiritual, and physical health.

When we find our inner voice, it is important to listen to it as a compassionate friend would—not judging what it tells us. Even if what we hear does not meet with our approval, it is only when we feel safe from our own criticism that what is inside us will emerge into the light of day. Then we can decide if what we discover there is something we want to nurture or transform. In this way we learn to trust our inner voice, have more choices in our behavior, and become more comfortable—and friendly—with ourselves.

In listening to the inner voice that reveals our personal truth, we can learn which parts of our external lives are satisfying and, conversely, which are destructive to our overall mental, emotional, spiritual, and physical health. If you are in a bad situation, the awareness of what that is costing you will generate the motivation to invent large or small ways of making it more tolerable or eventually getting out of it altogether. Remember, when we get to the end of our lives, we want to have as few regrets as possible about how we spent our time.

Thoughts and feelings are different sources of information, and each can turn up different conclusions. It's important that we learn to listen for the differences between the two. We can't arrive at personally appropriate answers until we can consciously include both what we think and what we feel in the equation. Gleaning the best from both of these, we can perceive the world with more understanding.

Unfortunately, it can be very difficult to include both because we live in a society that is biased toward rationality "uncontaminated" by emotion or intuition. In most areas of our adult lives, any public expression of emotion is viewed as a lack of control and casts doubt on our credibility. Unless you're on the front lines of a catastrophe involving death and starving children, shedding tears is probably not acceptable. You may remember Representative Pat Schroeder, who lost credibility when she shed tears in public. Having tested the waters for a presidential candidacy in 1989, Schroeder burst into tears and had to be comforted by her husband after she announced that she would not run. She had made this decision because she wanted to maintain personal contact with voters and was afraid that running for president would turn these contacts into little more than photo opportunities. After the announcement, she was written off by many as too emotional and not stable enough to be president, despite her track record of congressional leadership. In another example drawn from American presidential politics, Senator Edmund Muskie of Maine, the frontrunner in the 1972 Democratic presidential primary in New Hampshire, stood in the snow in front of the offices of the *Manchester Union Leader,* calling its publisher "a gutless coward" and appearing to weep in frustration and anger. The newspaper had published what is now known to have been a "Nixon dirty trick"—an attack accusing Muskie's wife of inappropriate behavior. Later Muskie said that that had been a pivotal moment, one that changed people's minds about his candidacy. Voters were looking for a strong, steady man, he said, but his expression of frustration and anger made them think he was weak. Providing a striking contrast is the example of John F. Kennedy's widow in the days following his assassination: Jackie Kennedy showed no emotion in public and was therefore lauded for her courage. As a society we were so ignorant of the emotional aftermath of sudden death that we didn't know that often the survivor is numb for a period of days, even months, and cannot feel anything at all. There is no doubt that Jackie Kennedy was a courageous woman by nature, but what our nation labeled as her courage in the weeks after the assassination was probably the numbness that comes of having experienced serious trauma.

Another important benefit of paying attention both to what we think and to what we feel is that we can catch those hardly heard, negative messages that our minds feed us, such as "I'm afraid I'm not good enough to do that job." How stupid I was to make that error, how bad my hair looks, how big my nose is, why didn't I notice that my socks don't match and no one will ever take me seriously again—these are messages that, most of the time, we are not even aware of, but they have an enormous negative impact on our self-esteem and confidence. When you practice listening to what your mind tells you, you get to decide which thoughts are supportive and which sabotage your efforts and sense of self-worth. Having decided which help and which hurt, you can reframe the negative messages so they no longer fog your perceptions and burden you with self-criticism. For instance, in one building in which I worked there was a stairwell with a blind corner. A mirror the full length and width of the blind wall had been installed so people could see if someone was coming either up or down the stairs toward them. I'd go to work and be feeling pretty good until my first trip down the stairs, when I would see myself in all my matronly, overweight glory. Seeing that image, I'd be flooded with thoughts of failure and feelings of shame that sometimes undermined my confidence for the rest of the day. Fortunately, I had learned the importance of listening to my thoughts. When I recognized the viciousness of this particular one, I reframed it from judgment to understanding. After that, whenever I went down the stairs and saw my reflection in the mirror, I remembered to think, "I would prefer not to look this way, but my work is so all-consuming that I have no time for any consistent form of nurture other than food." It wasn't long before this acceptance and less harsh observation of my appearance began to make a real difference. Eventually I could go down those stairs and see myself without a twinge, and sure enough, the self-loathing gradually disappeared. Listening to my thoughts, I was able to change them into accepting and supportive ones. Having the ability to make these changes helps us learn that we can trust ourselves for support even in difficult situations.

When we are able to know what is a thought and what is a feeling, we can live closer to our personal truth and be able to anticipate potential consequences of our actions. Being able to distinguish between our feelings and our thinking is essential to the ability to make choices based on our best knowledge, both intellectual and intuitive. When we acquire this skill, we are on our way toward wisdom. Wisdom is based in mind, spirit, heart, body, intuition, and experience. Wisdom is rare in our modern society, but it's an attribute that allows us to view life with clarity and acceptance. It is well worth working for.

When we really care about people, we listen to them. To care for ourselves—to become our best friend—requires that we listen to our own self, accepting what we find and paying particular attention to any self-criticisms that drag us down. When we become aware of these, we have the option of changing them into something more respectful and closer to the truth of who we are.

When, after nine years, I realized that my job as the sole counselor for an overwhelmingly large population at the retirement facility was draining all energy out of me, I resigned. I had loved being there; the work was very meaningful. But the job was too big for one person, and although I knew I would miss the people, I longed for the time and energy to have a life of my own. I wanted more opportunities to be with friends and attend cultural events. I wanted the luxury of paying attention to details, like mending clothes, doing laundry, painting a room, and reading good books.

Quitting my job was a risky move, but when I applied my standard measurement I knew that, for me, it was the right thing to do. The "standard measurement" that helps me make tough decisions is the question, "When I'm on my deathbed looking back on this time of my life, what will I want to see myself doing?" Danny Kwan, father of figure skater Michelle Kwan, has always taught his daughter that "the most painful thing to experience is not defeat, but regret."[2]

The loss of my steady income notwithstanding, it was a

healthy choice to leave my job. I still work—I write; I give lectures at conferences, seminars, and fund-raisers; I teach and develop new programs. Now that I have time to think, ideas and projects rise to consciousness as never before, and with them come excitement and the satisfaction of creating something new. Sometimes, of course, I am scared about the future. But this is the only life I have, and I want to live it.

So how much do we know about ourselves beyond our roles and careers? When you can no longer be the secretary, salesman, manager, nurse, homemaker, mother, CEO, physician, woodcarver, seamstress, marathon runner, or gardener you are now, then who will you be? Too many of us self-identify ourselves through our professional roles and recreational activities, never attaining an intimate relationship with who we are inside. Our sense of personal value depends on how closely we can conform to some popular image and to society's definition of success. On a superficial level this appears to work quite well while we're still functioning in the mainstream of life. But our roles and titles, our credentials, achievements, and possessions, are only the by-products of our effort. When these external identities fall away in late life, the self-esteem that depended on them will also disappear. The elders whose self-worth is based on these roles and expectations will have only the memories of who they have been and how much they have lost by which to define and experience their last years. Never having developed intimacy with themselves, they have no way of discovering the meaning of who they are. This creates a vacuum in the psyche in which emptiness and despair thrive.

Those who spend their lives avoiding the truth of themselves and the inevitability of their decline will find in late life that they have few skills for emotional self-support. Imagine being old and tired, living in a warp of timelessness. The days have little structure, so one day is pretty much like all the others; you can hardly tell if it's Monday or if it's Thursday. The future is a huge question mark—"Will I die tonight or ten years from now?" If you have severe physical limitations and are estranged from yourself and most of the people you know, you live with loneliness and dread as your only companions. If you still identify yourself by your old roles in active society, you have no positive or proactive ways to think about the disabled person you may have become. Your heart is heavy with its accumulated load of grief because you learned early to ignore its cry. If you are lucky, you have loving and competent care providers who connect with you and are an emotional life raft, but you are especially dependent on them because you never learned how to swim in deep waters yourself.

People who arrive at this stage of life with no emotional and spiritual preparation can find the experience so painful that they refuse to acknowledge the reality of their situation. They try to distance themselves from a lifetime's accumulated emotions, but these emotions, having been ignored, have now grown so large that they overwhelm the individual's coping skills. To protect themselves from this pain, people must numb themselves to feelings of any kind, including love. Having closed off their hearts and minds, they die long before their bodies do. Unfortunately, this is the experience of late life for many. It is important to recognize, however, that this living death is not an inevitable consequence of being old and chronically ill or disabled. Neither is it the result of a character flaw or weakness. It stems from a tragic lack of preparation.

Being our own friend means recognizing that we are not always going to be strong or right but that most of the time we are struggling to do the best we can. Often we'll be disappointed, even furious, with ourselves over something we've done that violates our values or standards or hurts someone we care about. Being a friend to ourselves means that we will learn to face our hard truths with compassion. Berating ourselves for mistakes we've made does not make up for what we've done, it just batters our self-esteem. When we can accept our imperfections with patience and kindness and are able to be honest about our errors, we can recognize the damage we've done and make repairs or amends in ways that won't belittle or diminish us. The confidence and increasing self-esteem that result from this practice will continue to grow and become a resilient internal strength. With this resilience we can cope better with the imperfections, disappointments, and losses of today, as well as those that will come at the end of our lives.

Being a best friend to yourself means that you hold the hopes and fears of your heart as sacred—never, ever belittling them. This respect for yourself ensures your knowing that in any situation, including your last years, you have both worth and substance.

Accepting the truth of both the good and the bad in ourselves is made more difficult by the influence of advertising on television, billboards, buses, cereal boxes, even our T-shirts—nearly everywhere we look. Advertising tells us what products will make us happy, satisfy our destiny, make us acceptable, exceptional, even desired. It tells us how we should look, how we should feel, and what we should be able to do if only we used a particular product. A pizza delivery truck states in big letters across both sides that its pizza is "the road to happiness!" It's a comfort food, no doubt about it, but does it really qualify as the road to happiness?

Personally, I deplore the ads that insist that if I used certain hair products, my fine, limp hair could be as long and thick as the model's. These ads caused feelings of failure in my younger years—even torture, if you consider the nights I spent sleeping in hair pins, brush rollers, or, worst of all, orange juice cans. Even though I came to recognize the hard sell, it has taken me decades to shake the feeling of being defective when I see that thick, flowing hair in the TV commercials. It's hard to keep these media images from creeping into our consciousness and becoming the standard by which we judge ourselves and define our worth. When we compare ourselves to the messages with which we are constantly bombarded, we may feel compelled to reject those parts of us that don't fit the commercially defined ideal.

Because of the sheer number of us who have reached middle age and above, the media are finally beginning to broaden their representation to include middle-aged and older people as well. They have finally begun to recognize that we are all market opportunities. But by far the image of youth is still the one we see most often. Youthful styles of clothing, makeup, and hair ignore the reality of those of us who are older and are having a darned hard time finding high-quality products that express mature good taste.

Our popular culture still does not acknowledge the depth of life after fifty, so what are we to think? That beyond these ages nothing of note happens, that we might as well not even exist? A nursing home resident told me she doesn't watch television because its overwhelmingly youthful and healthy images make her feel guilty and ashamed of being ninety years old and looking it. When will there be TV characters and shows that reflect a broader reality?

As long as I'm on the topic of media biases, passion and sex are nearly always shown as the exclusive territory of the young.

There's a big difference between lust and sensuous love. The young settle too easily for lust, mistaking the siren of sex for love. It takes decades to learn the latter, a more gentle form of passion and sensuality and one that not many of us would trade for the lust of our younger years. But because young lust is nearly all we see in movies and television, the assumption is that older people are not sexual, have no passion, and do not fall deeply in love. Here's the good news: if you grow yourself into a person who can love, age puts few limitations on love and sex. I officiated at the marriage of a couple in their eighties whose first joint purchase was a beautiful queen-size bed. In a nursing home I've seen genuine love and passion develop between people, and the staff members were respectful of their privacy because these residents, in their eighties and nineties, were sexually active. What a gift in our last years, to be cherished and loved both emotionally and physically!

If we are to be a friend to ourselves, we must pay attention to the warning that applies to every part of our body, spirit, and mind, which is, if we don't use it, we lose it. When you are old, don't expect to be in top form sexually if you've been celibate for many years. If you haven't exercised your spirit much, it's not going to be strong enough to support you. If you haven't pushed yourself to think and feel more deeply about life, including your own, or to nurture your curiosity and learn new things, then those faculties will be rusted shut by the time you reach old age. Your muscles will deteriorate if you don't use them; without exercise and calcium, your bones will become brittle. The disabling weakness that is the result of a nonexercised body is a common cause for admission into a nursing home. Being a couch potato—even when we're old—carries the high price of serious deterioration that could have been prevented. If we take care of our whole selves, we can reach old age and even chronic illness with some—or much—vitality left to us.

Remember early in this chapter I said that a good friend is someone who celebrates when we achieve something that is important to us? We must also learn to celebrate ourselves whether others do or not. Some of our achievements are not seen by other people, or their significance to us is not appreciated or understood by others. For instance, there may be no one who knows what it cost you in effort and courage just to get to where you are. There was that bully you survived in seventh grade, and all the Monday mornings you got up to go to a job you hated but couldn't afford to quit. How about all the nights you walked the floor with a colicky baby, and the years you went to night school after a full day's work so you could earn your degree? Think of the years you raised your children alone, or the decades you lived with the grief of knowing you would never have your own child, or the many times you had to explain and stand behind your decision not to have children. What about the times you had to work at a job while also caring for a sick family member?

Recall the crises you have already survived—the death of someone you love; a dream you finally discovered was not within your reach; divorce; financial stress; whatever events pushed you to the end of your emotional rope. Consciously honor what it took for you to hang on and get through those difficult and often devastating times. Acknowledge the strength it took, whether you felt strong at the time or not. You are a survivor. Take time to recall your achievements, especially the early ones that may no longer seem important (your current skills are based on these)—your educational degree; your Little League trophies; your first public speech; the craft award at the county fair; being honored for outstanding work on a science, corporate, school, or community project. These, too, are part of who you are—the work of your mind and hands and heart. This is not an exercise that includes comparing yourself to other people. What someone else has achieved is admirable but not fully knowable, just as what *you* have achieved is best understood by the one person who walks in your shoes and lives in your body: you.

Honoring yourself for what you have overcome and what you have achieved, taking time to name the specifics of these events, takes discipline in our busy, always-planning-for-the-future lives. But if you can cultivate an awareness of your strengths, your perseverance, your loyalty and commitment and just plain doggedness, you will gain the confidence of knowing what you can trust about yourself. This is an important stone in the foundation of self-respect and determines how we think of and treat ourselves. When we arrive at our last years, to a time when it might seem that we have little to offer the world, this self-knowledge will allow us to remember the whole of who we are and what our contributions to life have been. An awareness of the great effort and love we have poured into living will make it easier to accept the limitations that may eventually come to us.

Having this self-respect, honoring what we have faced, survived, and accomplished in our lifetime, will make it easier to accept that we cannot always be young and strong and that the lines and sags on our faces and bodies do not alter their worth or loveliness. We can choose to respect our lined faces for the laughter and tears that drew the maps on them, creating a beauty that no cosmetic surgeon can replicate. If some day we have painful, worn-out knees, we can remember how many places those knees have carried us—the lifetime average is 77,000 miles! When our knuckles are gnarled and veins and brown spots are the geography of our hands, we can think of all the things we've been able to do because of their dexterity, skill, and gentleness: the woodcarving, the needlework, the building of structures, the hanging of draperies and pictures that turned a house into a home. Remember especially how they soothed both feverish and grief-stricken brows, and think about how their caresses of love and kindness inspired and encouraged others.

Another important function of self-friendship is making a commitment to having nurturing and recreating activities as a regular part of our lives. Here again we have to listen to what our bodies and our internal selves are telling us about what we need. Our bodies try to let us know when we've been working too hard or are under too much stress. Even though we may not be listening, they give us early warning signs that we simply have to take time out to rest and recreate. If we continue to ignore those messages, they will become more strident until our bodies can no longer sustain our pace and we break down into illness.

When we are exhausted from too much work and too little play, every aspect of our lives suffers. The quality of our work and love is directly connected to the quality of our recreation. Balancing stressful activities with those that nourish us is key to our mental, emotional, spiritual, and physical health. Staying healthy is one of the most supportive and loving things we can do for ourselves. Learning self-care will have long-term benefits that will continue to sustain us in our last years.

Even though it may look easy to those of us still employed full-time, the stresses of late life can be the hardest ones of all. Not having employment to define the structure of our days can be a source of stress for those who are not comfortable with unstructured time. If we are not prepared for it by late life, our response to the unfamiliarity of unstructured time will be depression, apathy, frustration, and anger. Or we may respond by being compulsively busy with smaller and smaller details, a phenomenon I saw often among relatively healthy elders. I remember a poignant example from the retirement community I worked at. On one of the first balmy days of spring, the pink dogwoods were in full bloom, the azaleas were shining in their neon glory, the sun was giving depth and light to a full spectrum of green, and tiny songbirds shouted their gratitude from the trees and bushes. The open doors and windows in the hallways of the facility allowed the fragrant air to brush our skin indoors for the first time since the summer before. As I walked down a hallway, I passed two neighbors standing in their apartment doors talking to each other. One had already been out for the first of her several daily walks and was commenting on the beauty of the day. The other sighed and said, "Yes, I just wish I had time to go out and enjoy it." She had drawers to clean out, she explained. I walked down the stairs wondering how it could be that a retired person in her eighties, in relatively good health, with meals and house-keeping, laundry, and groundskeeping services provided, didn't have time for what the shut-ins—staff members and res-idents—would have given their collective right arm to enjoy! If this woman with clean drawers were to become disabled before she died, would she ever know how to live in the moment, or would she be preoccupied with what she should be doing and what she didn't get done? It's amazing to me what we can find to worry about when we have never learned to just "be" and live in the moment. Being our own friend means that when our bodies slow down, we must be able to be realistic about our limitations and our need for birdsong and balmy days.

Starting now, we can learn not to overwhelm and defeat ourselves by trying to live up to expectations we are not equipped for. Of course we should continue to set standards and challenges for ourselves so we can gain new information, understanding, and skills; what we won't do is set ourselves up for failure and self-loathing by believing that we are supposed to have all the answers and be able to perform all jobs and activities with the dexterity we had in our thirties, forties, and fifties. When activities make our aging bodies feel as if they've been tortured, it's time to hire out the work or ask for help—or get off the couch and get in better shape!

We can arrive at our last stage already expert at realistic adaptation and acceptance and with the ability to receive assistance. We will have learned patience with our imperfections, trusting ourselves to do the best we can when our aging bodies cannot live up to standards that are no longer possible for us. Then we will be able to ease into whatever changes our old age brings with fairly short-lived grief for all but the biggest losses. The early practice of adjusting to the small changes that begin to occur in middle age will help us cope with the radical changes old age will bring. Healthy adaptation will enable us to remain emotionally and spiritually vital despite any physical or cognitive limitations.

In late life, knowing yourself well enough to know what you need is the only way you will be able to hold your ground in the face of hierarchical care-providing systems. Anyone who has worked in a medical setting knows that the pecking order is harsh and that territoriality is fierce. There are medical personnel who are exceptions, of course, but my own experience working in these settings is that a majority of professionals hold the firm belief that they know what's right for you, regardless of what you think. If we cannot clearly state our preferences and needs and negotiate our situation—standing our ground with emotional strength—the likelihood is that others will make the decisions that affect us. And even the care providers who are compassionate and caring by nature often find it hard to appreciate the nuances of being old and tired. They tend to be younger, and often they have been better trained at "doing" than at "listening." While they may mean well, their agenda will not always be the same as ours. If we cannot speak for ourselves in the face of their power, we will lose our own. When we lose our power and our choices are few, we feel helpless. Powerlessness and helplessness are feelings that drag us into passivity or hostility, both of which are self-perpetuating. The more passive we become, the more helpless and hopeless we feel. Likewise, the more hostile we become, the more frustrated and helpless we feel. Only those of us who come to these last years with self-respect and an intimate knowledge of what we need can guide and inform those who are assigned to assist us. In this way we can maintain dignity and control, or at least increase the possibility of being heard and respected by both professional service providers and our own family members.

It takes a long time to grow into being your own best friend; it takes years of trial and error, of growing trust and acceptance of yourself. If you are fortunate, you have several close friends, but still you need to be your own friend. It can save you from heartbreaking loneliness. After all, if you live long enough, you may outlive every friend except yourself.

The family of eighty-eight-year-old Eunice moved her from her old house and neighborhood to a new double-wide in a beautifully landscaped mobile home retirement community. Her new home was one level and so were the sidewalks, a seemingly welcome change from the ones in her old neighborhood, lifted and broken by the roots of old trees. Here she would be safer, less isolated, closer to her family. They took her shopping, to her doctor's appointments, and out to dinner at least once a week. Two generations checked in and watched out for her every day. But when I visited with her, Eunice talked of her loneliness. She had outlived every person she knew of her generation—family, friends, even acquaintances. Although her worried children and grandchildren urged her to go to the recreation center where she could meet new friends, she would not go. Eunice had a chronic illness that forced her to stay home most of the day and kept her in a state of exhaustion. Her young family members were perplexed, having had no experience of how much energy it takes to meet new people when one is old, ill, and tired. They didn't realize that there was no way for Eunice to convey to strangers her eighty-eight-year history, no way to make up for the fact that none of these new people had known her beloved husband. She grieved the loss of her old friends who had known him and who had known her strengths and achievements in those years when she'd had stamina and energy. She no longer had any peer with whom she could share personal memories.

When you have lived almost an entire lifespan, with all of its details and crises and triumphs, how do you begin to introduce yourself to strangers? There is so much you could tell them about yourself! Where do you start? What do you leave out? How much will they be willing to hear? And will you have enough energy to figure it out and carry through? Some people in the last stage of their lives can and do develop close relationships with peers they have recently met. But what I have observed overall is that many new friendships made in late life are kept on a fairly superficial level. There is just too much history for each person to share, and no way to convey adequately the personal impact of important events.

If some day toward the end of our life we should find ourselves in the situation that Eunice was in, with all or most of our aged peers dying before we do, then having long-term friends who are younger than we are will mean a lot in our need for human connection. It is in the sharing of memories that we are reminded of who we have been and who we still are. Look at your circle of friends, keeping the future as well as the present in mind. Are they all about your age, or do you have younger friends as well? Many of those younger friends may still be around to accompany us in our last stage of life.

I learned the importance of having a shared history and memories with friends when I took my first placement as a parish minister. It involved moving to a different city, one in which I didn't know another soul. Within four days of my arrival I had preached my first sermon, and thereby one hundred people knew me professionally. But it was more than a year before I had a friend, someone with whom I could just be myself.

That first year, when I had recognition but no close friends, was very difficult and lonely. Some mornings I wept at the idea of having to face another day. I thought longingly of the friends I'd left behind who'd known me well enough to remind me when I was feeling bad that I'd be fine the next day. They knew what I was capable of and in what circumstances I needed their moral support. They knew of my hard work and achievements, both the large and the small ones. They knew the effort it had taken me to get through graduate school as a single mother. They had been at my ordination service and participated in my first official serving of communion. Not only did they know the personal me and what I had accomplished, but they trusted me and liked my imperfect self. I never had to put up a front with them.

The people in my new community didn't have any sense of my history besides what they'd seen on my résumé and what they had learned in two interviews. Since I needed to make a good impression, I couldn't afford to let them see anything but my best foot forward. Even on my day off, I had to be ready to be friendly and empathic at the grocery store, the bank, and the dry cleaner's because I was the-minister-of-the-church-down-the-block, and nothing less was expected. I was sure I would die of terminal "niceness." I would have given anything for a day off in which I could whine and complain with a good friend to listen. I was perpetually exhausted and constantly criticizing myself for not being as strong as I appeared to be.

Like so many people who work long and hard to achieve their dreams, I had ignored the needs of my heart and body for nurture and recreation. I had little experience of caring for myself, and I didn't have a clue about the importance of being my own friend. Like elders who have outlived their old friends, I had no one in this new place who appreciated my history and all that had gone into making me who I was.

As difficult as this experience was, it served me well when I left the parish ministry and realized I had no social life. Years of working sixty to eighty hours per week as well as being a single parent had left me with no opportunities for socializing outside of my professional role. I thought of Eunice, who had outlived all of her peers, and decided I needed a plan. I knew I required solitude and time with my son. That didn't leave much for socializing, so I decided to be very selective about whom I would spend this precious time with. Long-term, close relationships always involve some maintenance, such as making sure not too much time passes from one visit or call to the next, and taking time to work through conflicts as they arise. I wanted these investments of my time with people to count. I began to think in terms of which friends I'd want at my hundredth-birthday party—which was then only fifty-two years away. Whom did I want to know for that long? I began intentionally building a circle of friends who enhanced my life in the present and who might have the commitment and staying power for long-term friendship. Having learned firsthand the importance of being with friends who share one's history, I included in the circle people who were fifteen years younger than I am (now, more than a decade later, my circle of friends has grown to include men and women who are twenty and thirty years younger than me!). They are mature, bright, and interesting, and I hope that some day, when I can no longer drive or am home- or institution-bound, they will come see me and share news and laughter as well as memories.

Life being what it is, there is no guarantee that even my young friends will outlive me. If I respect and know myself, listening for my own truth, I can accept myself with kindness and appreciate what it has taken to be me. I can learn what I want and what I need, and I can learn how to ask for them. Having these skills in my last years will make it easier to reconcile myself to whatever limitations I may have and to treat myself with the self-respect each of us deserves.

Having all this, I know that I will never be—at least not to myself—an anonymous old woman.

# 2

# Learning to Grieve

When the pioneers packed for the trip west, they included items that had made their lives pleasurable: the huge, ornate trunk that had crossed the Atlantic; the beautiful pump organ the family gathered around on Sunday evenings; Aunt Sally's trunk of beautiful dresses (since she wasn't married yet); Mother's collection of cut glass; Grandpa's hand-carved chair and bedstead; trunks of hand-decorated linens; beautiful hand-painted oil lamps. Many of these were found along the road in later seasons by other people. The heavy trunks were left at river crossings; the beautiful old organs made it only halfway up the mountainsides; the linens, the glassware, the hand-carved furniture had made the wagon loads too heavy and bulky for the difficult terrain in which the people found themselves. The pioneers had to leave things behind so they could make progress. Those who insisted on keeping everything they started out with were the ones most likely to drown in the river's currents, to get trapped in the mountains in winter, or to stop short of their destination. So it is, beginning in middle age and up into late life: those things we can't imagine living without will all, eventually, be left at the side of the road.

Some years ago I unrolled a long strip of shelfpaper and mapped out on it what I thought I'd like to be doing professionally in another two to three years and the steps that might get me there. I had no desire to leave the facility where I was counseling elder clients, since I loved that work; so in fact I had no idea how any change could happen—it was a product of pure hope. The first step, taking better care of myself (I was perpetually exhausted in those days), seemed so ordinary and obvious that I didn't feel particularly encouraged by embarking on it; it didn't give me the feeling of actually making any concrete progress toward the long-term changes I dreamed of.

It was about this time that I read that the crow is an omen of change in some Native American lore. Having read that, I began to notice for the first time how numerous crows are in this part of the country. I was looking for anything that might signal my hope for change as being possible, so I decided to make the crow an encouraging omen, like a star to wish on. Whenever my eye caught sight of a crow, I told myself it meant something new was on the horizon. A friend pointed out that there were crows everywhere; how could they possibly be meaningful? Yes, I told her, but I don't actually look for them, I just notice the ones that put themselves in my line of vision, like the one sitting right there at eye level on the brick wall in front of my friend and me. And seeing that crow I felt a surge of hope and thought, "A change is coming."

In the years since I learned that bit of crow lore, my professional life has taken some surprising and challenging turns. I don't give crows credit for these twists and turns any more than I would a star I had wished on, but I'm grateful for the little surges of hope that kept me going whenever I noticed one.

Along with the hope that change might bring come the adjustments to a new reality. Around our fiftieth birthday, an invitation to join AARP arrives in the mail and we realize with a jolt that we're only ten or fifteen years away from retirement![3] Maybe we won't reach our professional goals after all, or make our first million, or have a child, or run a four-minute mile. A forty-seven-year-old contractor notes with regret that he can't jump between the beams of his construction projects with the same balance and agility he enjoyed in earlier years. A lifelong hiker in her sixties finds she now needs a hand to steady her when she crosses streams she's not willing to fall into. We realize with annoyance and even shame that most fashionable, good-quality clothing is designed for bodies twenty and thirty years younger than ours. Young adults frequently don't notice our presence even when we stand in the same room with them. Those of us with children have waved good-bye to them as they've launched themselves into the world. Wandering through the now silent house, we miss their raucous and often irritating presence and wonder what the prudent timing is for converting their rooms to a study or a sewing or arts room. Some of us are back in the hospital delivery room, only this time waiting for the birth of a grandchild. Another day we go for an eye exam, learn that we have progressed to bifocals or trifocals, and are chagrined that our glasses have become more than just a fashion statement. We have begun to receive unaccustomed respect from people we assumed were peers, until we notice with a start that, only in our fifties, we are the oldest couple at the faculty party! An elder friend told me how startled he was when he received an invitation to join the club reserved for people who had worked for his corporation for twenty-five years. When he was hired to work there, he said, the members of the twenty-five-year club were the oldest people he knew! Now that I look matronly, store clerks who've been trained to notice the names on customers' credit cards refer to me as "Mrs.," an assumption that baffles and irritates me. In the early 1970s I worked hard for the right to be identified as "Ms." rather than by marital status; besides, I've been single more than twenty years. Most shocking of all is the fact that some of the professionals I consult are young enough to be my children!

It is incomprehensible that we are no longer young, impossible that we are on our way to being old. We stay busy keeping one step ahead of the knowledge that we are losing ground in some of the areas we have most identified ourselves with. We increase our time at the gym, step up from Revlon to Estée Lauder, consult a cosmetic surgeon, and go on new diets. Some days—if we haven't had our face lifted—we avoid our reflection in the mirror.

We can, and many of us do, try to ignore the reality of our aging. Using my younger self, who could do almost anything, as my standard, I can push myself beyond my current levels of endurance and stamina. I could give up the quiet pursuits that now nurture me and spend more hours at the gym. But while I work to keep my life in suspended animation, everything—including me—is in a process of change. The universe continues to expand, the ice caps at the poles are melting, the texture of my skin shows nearly sixty years of living, the thousands of miles I've walked are etched into my feet and knees, and somewhere along the way I slipped over the line from being protégé to mentor. In thoughtful moments I can see the end of the tunnel where death awaits me, and I know that my list of what's relevant at that time will be a very short one. Now when I see a crow, I am reminded that change is the only constant in life.

With every change there is a loss of the familiar. Even if it is a familiar we dislike, it's part of the structure that defines our days and offers stable reference points. Say a promotion finally comes through and you move to a new branch to take up other duties. The salary increase allows you to obtain housing you could only dream of in earlier years. You're stimulated by the new challenges and what the future holds. You've finally "made it," or are in the fast lane to getting there. But in the early stages of these good changes, you sometimes feel crabby, tired, and depressed. Your moodiness makes no sense at all in the context of your good fortune. But in the deeper layers of your consciousness you are missing familiar routines, places, co-workers—maybe you're even feeling a bit of nostalgia for the one you always thought was a jerk. The new routines are different and you miss Tuesday breakfast with your former partner. You haven't found a dry cleaner or a dentist yet, and the food-stocking arrangement at the local supermarket is still baffling. When I moved to take the job that I'd been dreaming about and preparing for for years, my breaking point came with the morning newspaper. I'd been doing quite well in my new home and job for several months (although admittedly I was crabby, tired, and depressed when no one was around to see), but one morning I sat down at the kitchen table with my coffee and the newspaper and unexpectedly began to weep. The paper wasn't the *San Francisco Chronicle,* which I'd read every day for eighteen years. I didn't like the layout of this unfamiliar paper, didn't know its columnists or where to find important things like my horoscope. It was the last straw; I sat at the table and mourned the loss of the stable events that had defined the world and my place in it. Even this good change, for which I had worked so long and hard, carried within it pockets of loss and grieving until I had time to realign myself to the new reality and let go of the old. In any moving forward, there is always a leaving behind.

Imagine, then, the impact on us when our roles, status, physical abilities, and appearance begin to reflect the normal changes brought about by aging. If we have enjoyed the status of any professional role, if we have identified ourselves with what we can do or how young we look or with how others view us, then it's going to be hurtful and disorienting when these are altered. How much we are hurt and disoriented will depend on how much we've identified ourselves with these roles, abilities, and appearances, and whether the change is the first age spot on our face or the death of someone we love.

My first experience of the sometimes shocking changes age brings occurred one Saturday morning when I drove my son to his high school to catch the bus that would take him to the ski slopes of Mount Hood for the day. His excitement electrified the atmosphere of our station wagon, loaded down with his duffel bag, lunch, skis, and poles. When we arrived at the schoolyard I got a swift "Bye" as he swept his gear out of the car and headed for the bus, pausing to exchange tough-guy greetings with his friends. They were raring to go: their agenda was fast-moving thrills and all-day flirtation. I thought of the sting of fresh air on cold cheeks and the satisfying, bone-deep exhaustion of having played hard in nature's beauty. I was envious of my son.

By the time I got home, my mood had plummeted, the day and the house had grown dark. I'd lost energy and any enthusiasm I'd had for this rare occasion, a day on my own. I mumphed around the house, griping to myself. And then I listened to what I was doing and recognized it—loss. This was not just a bad mood, not just grouchiness, it was loss I was feeling. My son was doing what I had always planned to do. Lack of money and long work hours had occupied the years between youth and middle age. I could still try it—after all, I was only fifty and I occasionally went cross-country skiing—but I had to acknowledge that running my nonathletic body down the ski slopes was taking a 50–50 chance that it would end in a ride straight to the hospital. I decided I wasn't willing to risk it. Sadness replaced my foul mood. I didn't like the grief any more than I liked the earlier mood, but at least these feelings made sense. I wept a little and let the waves of sadness move through me. I realized that there was a timeliness to this, that this is what begins to happen in middle age, and that it would not be the last time I would have to let something go. Our lives are a series of losses that begin even as we gain the high ground of middle age.

Those black balloons and "Over the Hill" birthday napkins suggest that we've either passed or will soon be passing the peak of our climb. But more and more of us are enjoying an extended hike across a high plateau before we reach the slope that will take us down the other side. Traveling down off the high ground is a bit like mountain climbing. The first step often involves the terrifying process called rappelling. This has to be one of the most heart-stopping experiences that a beginning climber has to face. First you lean back in a body harness held by an impossibly small rope attached to a stake or wrapped around someone's waist, and then you step backward off the edge of the cliff into thin air. This kind of "letting go"—stepping off and letting yourself down the rope to the next ledge—is pure joy for the experienced and pure terror for the beginner. I remember the terror well. It was stolid resignation that got me into that harness: I had a lot of face to save and no other way off the mountain. I buckled on the harness; the rope was threaded through the proper carabiners and around the waist of the person who would pay out the line as I went over the edge and dropped down the face of the cliff. All I had to do was lean back and, holding the rope, step off the edge. I did it; I took that awful step. Once over the edge, I found the experience exhilarating. The next opportunity I had to rappel was a more willful letting go, leaning back, stepping off, hanging in midair with the knowledge that the next ledge would appear under me eventually.

As with rappelling, the first indication that we're aging—that we're at the edge of the down slope or the cliff—can be unbelievable and demoralizing. But with practice at reconciling ourselves to what has to be, we can lean into the experience that will carry us to the next ledge. Reconciliation is the only way we can move to the next level with any confidence. Traveling down the far side of the hill is another step in our human journey, and it will take us to another vantage point. We may be challenged by the terrain, but the view will be new, presenting its own interesting beauty.

One thing our culture is stupefyingly ignorant about is loss—its effect on us, ways of coping with it, and ways of talking about it. Expression of our grief is the only way we can move through it and get on with our lives. Few people and even fewer corporations appear to have much knowledge about the effects of loss on the human being.[4] On the whole, our society has lost the knowledge of endings. Endings—especially "unhappy" ones—make us nervous. Many people, including those in the field of science, view old age and death as problems to be cured. Bigger, better, and more is the unwritten mission statement of most of contemporary society. We don't know how to acknowledge the demise of things: we talk of "failure" and "losers" when speaking of a business that has died or an individual who has fallen on hard times. We use euphemisms for physical death, such as "We lost her" or "He passed on." The words "died" or "death" are treated as obscenities, not to be spoken in polite company.

The less dramatic losses of middle age are ignored. In fact, we are encouraged to work and play harder. A "Health Report" in *Time* magazine noted that "men who consistently jog 40 miles or more a week still put on pounds as they age— about 3.3 lbs. per decade, plus about 3/4 of an inch on their waistlines. How to avert the girth? Tack on more and more miles each year."[5]

The devastation of a major loss—perhaps the death of a spouse, a child, or a best friend—is even less understood. In the business world, when an immediate family member of an employee dies, most companies will allow seventy-two hours for grieving and attending the funeral. A banker friend once told me of his frustration and puzzlement over the mental paralysis of a man who had been a key player in his department. This colleague had been the creative force behind a major idea the bank wanted to incorporate into its services. When the man's child died, the bank had given him a generous three weeks off. But six months later, although he was showing up for work every day, there was little sign of his former creativity and follow-through, and the project had come to a standstill. No one understood what had happened to him or knew what to do about it. They did not know that the emotional crisis of the bereaved father had left him unable to concentrate or to care much about anything. He was so parched of heart and mind that creativity would not be forthcoming for another year or two—or maybe not ever, unless he could allow himself to actively grieve. Many bereaved people have expressed to me a longing to keen and wail their losses as uninhibitedly as the people of some other cultures do, but they find no place here where that behavior is acceptable.

If we as a society don't recognize and offer appropriate long-term support to those trying to recover from a major loss, we are certainly not prepared to acknowledge the facts and consequences of the small losses that begin in middle age. If I had not recognized my bad mood as an experience of loss the day I dropped my son off to go skiing, I would have berated myself all day for being lazy or having a bad attitude, and perhaps I would even have sunk all the way to the point where I would have been questioning my right to occupy space on the planet. As it was, the recognition didn't make the day much more fun, but it allowed me to express feelings appropriate to the situation, rather than machine-gunning myself psychologically for not living up to my standards of behavior and mood. And by recognizing the reality and allowing myself to feel and express the loss, I was engaged in a process of healing and letting go. It took a few weeks for me to realize for certain that I'd reached some kind of turning point, but whenever I had the image of myself skiing downhill at a high speed and totally out of control, I realized again that the experience was something I would never have. Each time I was reminded of the loss it was a little less painful until finally there was no emotional charge to the recognition at all. In no way do I intend to indicate this particular loss as universal; there are people in their eighties and nineties on ski slopes doing just fine. It's only an example of one loss to one middle-aged person.

We may find ourselves restless and grumpy at times and

not know why. It's likely that the source of these mood states is unrecognized and unexpressed sadness caused by changes, including those that come with aging. One doesn't have to look far to find a reason to feel bad about these alterations of our selves, at least the physical ones. For instance, while most women I know don't care how much hair a man has, he is told every day by advertisements on TV, radio, billboards, magazines, and newspaper that a full head of hair would make him look younger and sexier. According to the ads, getting more hair can be achieved by joining a hair club, having hair plugs put in the scalp, surgically lifting the scalp and pulling it forward, or—I especially like this one—using spray paint to create the illusion of hair instead of a bald spot. A woman in her late eighties told me that some television commercials are downright frightening to her: they insist that you buy their product *right now,* and they provide a twenty-four-hour 800 number so you don't spend *another minute* succumbing to the effects of age. The sense of urgency is alarming: how can any of us develop a positive attitude toward aging if the commercials are telling us that it's a crisis, a disaster, something to be nipped in the bud immediately?

Preteen models set the standard for beauty, despite the fact that those of us who are entering middle or old age possess a textured beauty that only experience can etch onto our bodies and faces. As for me, it's the old faces I pick out in a crowd. Having related to elders professionally and personally for many years, I find their faces far more interesting and attractive than those of the young with their bland beauty.

Those of us who live in industrialized societies have enviable powers and choices. That we have so much at our disposal and under our control makes us exquisitely vulnerable to despair and shame when we lose it. Research shows that people with a strong belief in their ability to control what happens have more difficulty when the losses of life occur. They have a harder time coping than those who have learned and reconciled themselves to the fact that there are some things that are simply beyond their control.[6] If we insist on trying to maintain a status quo that no longer exists, we are sure to create feelings of failure that sabotage our self-esteem. For the past five years I have had to keep reminding myself that no matter how many hours I spend on my treadmill or lifting weights, I will never regain my thirty-five-year-old body. If I can't release the physical standard of my thirty-five-year-old self for one more appropriate to my age, I can only experience defeat, no matter how much I work out. Threats to our self-esteem contribute to the sometimes frantic, even self-destructive behaviors of some midlife crises, such as a husband's or a wife's trying to recapture the lust of youth with an adulterous affair, or our spending money beyond our means on artifacts or procedures that promise happiness and the recapturing of youth. Middle age is also a time in which parents may slip into competitiveness with their children because they can't acknowledge their aging. Rather than allowing our offspring to take their rightful place of ascendancy, we may try to outdo them to maintain an outdated self-identity and remain in the more powerful position. A classic case is the athletic father who drives himself to beat his grown son at sports and then loudly gloats about it. Another is the mother who flirts with her daughter's date, or one who tries to run her grown daughter's household in an attempt to prove that she still has the greater knowledge and power. This is a dangerous time if we continue to insist that we can do as much as or more than younger people; we may push ourselves into workaholism or athletic competition beyond our stamina and burn out or otherwise injure ourselves. When this happens, we become disappointed and vulnerable to feelings of failure and depression; and our children, whom we have bested, feel diminished and insulted.

Since, as a society, we don't recognize the emotional cost of loss, individuals who find themselves in the middle of it frequently have little understanding of what is happening to them and why they feel so out of control emotionally. In our busy, middle-aged lives we leave many things, events, and people—including ourselves—unexamined. Assuming they'll always be the same, we have no curiosity about them. We fill our roles, do what's expected of us, behave normally, and sail across life without ever really being *in* it. "Sailing across life" doesn't mean we never feel pain, but that somehow we don't manage to do more than skip across the surface. We never reach very far beneath or beyond what society or family and friends expect of us. This way we can exist very comfortably for a while; there are no surprises, no risks, and therefore no unusual amounts of effort to expend. Not a lot of energy has to go into thinking things out because we've already figured out as much as we have to, to keep the status quo. But this experience, of course, is based on the illusion that things don't change—the assumption that our favorite television show will always be aired, that our car will stay new, that our favorite restaurant will never close, and that neither we nor the people we know will ever die. When these changes do take place, when the bottom is jerked out from under our previously predictable lives, we are stunned, shocked, outraged, and inconsolable, depending on the magnitude of the change. If by middle age we have not anticipated these changes, especially the major ones, many of us may never regain our equilibrium when they occur.

Mustering the courage to face the coming alterations of

age and our own mortality, we can begin to learn the art of grieving. Paradoxically, learning to grieve also enables us to let go and be "in" our lives in a very different, more satisfying way. When we know that something is temporary, we tend to relate to it in a more conscious way than we do when we believe it will always be there.

If I am traveling in a foreign country, or if a doe and her fawn appear in front of me, I am more alert and attentive to details than when I am in situations I take for granted. One of the few events that can get most people's attention is a spectacular sunset. A sunset doesn't last long, and if we don't stop and appreciate it right now, it'll be gone. Yes, there will be others, but a truly spectacular one gives those who stop to see it the experience of just "being there" in the moment, taking in the beauty even as it fades. If we can keep the temporary nature of things in mind, we are less likely to take them for granted and more likely to enjoy their beauty and their meaning to us.

There is something about knowing that virtually nothing is permanent, including our abilities and our lives, that opens us to truly seeing and experiencing things, taking them into ourselves and pondering larger meanings. When I was interning as a hospital chaplain, I met a young mother who was dying of cancer. She said to me, "If I could tell people anything, I would tell them to really look at things, really look at them! Like the tree outside my hospital window—I think God made the crotch in that tree just so that squirrel could sit in it." Another wonderful example comes to mind from a later time, during my years working at the retirement community. A resident came into the building from the gardens carrying a beautiful tomato she'd grown herself. When she arrived at the elevators that would take her to her apartment, the tomato caught the eye of another resident, whose disabilities prevented her from doing her own gardening or even going outside very often. Together the two of them sat and studied the red fruit, taking turns holding it and turning it around and around in their hands. They commented on the smooth feel of the skin, the rich, deep color of the fruit, the unsurpassed flavor of a tomato ripened in one's own garden. This reminded them of gardens past, so they shared a few amusing stories of weeding and harvesting their mothers' gardens and talked about how good the tomatoes had still tasted, reharvested in the dead of childhood winters from the jars in which they had been canned. By now the two women had missed several elevators, but appreciating the miracle of a tomato and sharing the memories it stirred was so pleasurable to both that they told me about it weeks later.

When I found I no longer had the stamina to work long hours clearing the fallen limbs in the woods around my house, I began to bring a lawn chair and a thermos with me. I still work in the woods, but stop frequently to sit and have a cup of tea. I've identified birds I didn't know lived here and evidence that a bobcat shares the property. Since I've slowed down some, I see things I never saw before and find that quiet solitude is not lonely but nurturing, allowing my heart to open to the signs and lessons of nature that surround me.

When we learn to recognize the subtle and not-so-subtle changes that begin to occur in midlife, when we acknowledge their impact on how we feel about ourselves, when we learn to name the pockets of sadness and grief for what they are and allow their expression, then we are in a process of healing and flowing with the transitions, letting go of what has been and can no longer be. Only then are we freed to turn our faces toward a new shore where we may discover possibilities that are richer and deeper than any we've had access to before.

The importance of learning to grieve and let go applies to grudges as well. If we hang on to them, they can eventually extract a very high price. I think of a woman at the retirement facility named Eleanor, who told me she had caught her son's wife in a compromising situation soon after the wedding. Although Eleanor would never say exactly what the situation was, she had never forgiven her daughter-in-law. She had, in fact, been so openly judgmental that family gatherings became impossibly conflicted. Finally she confronted her son and demanded that he choose between herself and his wife. He chose his wife. After that rejection, Eleanor did not go to a family gathering or see her son or his family for over twenty years. She allowed only a distant cousin to be her "family." Eventually, but grudgingly, Eleanor allowed her grown grandchildren to contact her, and thus began a series of regular visits. Over time she grew to love and admire their personalities, their integrity, their obvious affection for her. They went to great lengths to bring her back into the family, but Eleanor would still not go anywhere their mother might be. Eleanor wasn't moved one iota when I pointed out to her that it had been fifty years since the indiscretion and that perhaps she might credit her daughter-in-law for the longevity of her marriage and the raising of four fine children. Stubbornly, she would not budge from her ivory tower of disapproval.

When Eleanor's physical and mental health seriously deteriorated, the grandchildren wanted to care for her, but the distant cousin, whom Eleanor had come to distrust and dislike, petitioned for an involuntary guardianship and would not even allow them to visit her. When Eleanor died she was alone, and only the cousin was notified. What a sobering way for me to learn that grudges are a luxury only the young can afford!

Some relationships are so toxic, however, that you cannot make them work, no matter how hard you try. You may eventually have to break off such a relationship in order to keep your own sanity. This is especially gut-wrenching when the relationship is with someone you love, maybe even family. If you ever have to do this with someone you care deeply about, be prepared for a long stretch of grieving. Ultimately the pain of the loss will come to an end and you will be healthier and happier for having eliminated the stress.

Preserving your sanity in this way is not the same as carrying a grudge or fighting to maintain the more powerful position. Grudges and holding ourselves superior are what cause us problems at the end of life, when we realize that we've wasted years controlling or judging someone we might otherwise have enjoyed and loved. A grudge is fed by self-righteousness, which can feel awfully good because it hides insecurity. It allows us to feel imagined superiority over someone we want to cut down to a size we're more comfortable with. A grudge is something no one can take away from you because it's your decision to have it. For a grudge-filled elder, the old echoes of self-righteousness still hint at imagined power. Right up to her lonely end, Eleanor would toss her head disdainfully whenever the subject of her daughter-in-law came up.

Grudges require a tremendous amount of energy to maintain, which may be the reason why, when we grow old and tired, they've become more habit than anything else. Sometimes elders can't even remember why they carried disapproval for so many years, but to admit they've been wrong when they're already losing everything seems to be more than most people can muster.

By middle age, as we look down the road and make choices that will maintain meaning and love into our last years, it's time to search ourselves for the large and small angers we harbor. Some angers may already have diminished and be relatively easy to let go of; other angers may have grown from a lot of pain that was caused by another person, and may now be so large and all-encompassing that it will take more effort and time—even years—to let go of them. Do it for yourself, do it for your present peace of mind, and do it for your future.

Middle age is the time when we mark the end of our child-rearing days; when we may ponder for the first time the roads we didn't take; when we realize we can't go back and relive the happy times or undo the bad ones. Middle age is when we are most likely to begin experiencing the major losses of grandparents and parents and the untimely losses of good friends, a sibling, a spouse, even children. These latter losses overwhelm us with the reality of the unthinkable and a profound sense of injustice. I was pondering this one morning in my house, which sits high on the side of a hill. Seen from outside, the large windows reflect the sky and surrounding trees. Birds, seeing nothing threatening ahead, sometimes fly straight into the windows. Some are lucky and fly away, but others don't survive the impact. That morning I heard a thump against the living room window and stepped out onto my deck, dreading what I would find. There lay a little finch with wing and body angles so unnatural that I knew he would not be able to fly away. As I held him in my palm, his shiny black eyes turned dull with the film of death. I felt sorrow for the abrupt ending of this beautiful little life and frustration that the home that is a sanctuary for me is an instrument of death for the birds. Pondering this paradox, I realized this is what life is like, no more, no less. Any being, human or otherwise, can be doing exactly what it is intended to be doing, flying through the trees and into the sky, seeing only more of the same ahead, when WHAM!—without warning, it crashes into an unseen wall, and life as it knows it is over or irrevocably changed. The loss of a job, a divorce, a diagnosis of chronic or terminal illness, the deaths of loved ones—depending on the significance to us of the thing or person lost, the aftermath can range from mild debilitation to outright devastation.

Sadness and grief do not take place in the territory of the rational mind, they are a function of the heart. Our rational minds may understand and accept the change but be unable to make the feelings disappear. Feelings are powerful, affecting much more than our mood; sadness and grief impact the physical body as well. Some physical symptoms of grief are loss of appetite or overeating, insomnia, extreme fatigue, heartache, heavy sighing, stomach and digestive problems, a lump in the throat, sweating, nausea, pain, sensitivity to noise, impaired reflexes, prolonged and unexpected weeping. It may hurt to breathe or swallow, and one's skin may even hurt. Grief can depress the immune system, making the bereaved person more vulnerable to illness.

The emotional and mental components of loss can include unusual worrying, anxiety and fear, irritability, confusion, feeling more easily hurt, loss of interest, intense loneliness, poor concentration (a person might read the same line over and over and still not comprehend what it says), and poor memory. One woman I know, grieving over her divorce, absentmindedly put her gym shoes in the refrigerator and then spent the morning scolding her dog for having hidden them. She felt pretty silly when she opened the refrigerator later that day and found her shoes next to the orange juice.

Some of us, if we are able to, become obsessively busy with work when we feel the stirrings of sadness, loss, or grief, because grief is so darned painful and the experience of loss makes us feel so helpless. Staying busy is often a way of trying to regain control of our lives and feelings, and for many it's an effective coping mechanism. If our flurry of activity prevents us, however, from feeling the sadness that our body and psyche need to release, we may numb all feelings, including those of contentment, love, or caring about anything, and slip into a low-grade or full-blown depression instead.

Our consumer frenzy is largely fueled by repressed losses, disappointments, fear, and feelings of powerlessness. We purchase items to fill emotional vacuums: buying gives us the illusion of power and control. Temporarily sating our sadness, emptiness, or boredom, buying is an activity we are encouraged from all sides to engage in.

But grief doesn't go away. It's a stressful event, and if we don't release some of that stress, it will take its toll on our bodies, our mental health and life satisfaction. What's more, it will sit and wait until we can no longer maintain our busyness. Then, when we have to slow down or come to a stop, it will rise to the surface. It will also come out when another loss occurs—we will feel not only the pain of the current loss but the accumulated grief of past losses as well. This happened to ninety-year-old Rose, who had just moved to the nursing home and found that she could not speak of her brother without weeping. She was perplexed and embarrassed by her uncontrollable tears because he had died so many decades earlier, when he was five and Rose was only three. But the two of them had been inseparable in those first few years of their lives, and in the year following his death, an unspeakable event for little Rose, she had been completely mute. Now, triggered by the loss associated with her move into the nursing home, the tears she had not shed as a child were finally flowing.

Grief trapped in the heart causes suffering. We may learn to coexist with its discomforts while we're still busy and mobile, but when late life brings us to a standstill, we will have few ways to protect ourselves from the tidal wave of accumulated grief and remorse. It will crash upon the shore of our psyche and destroy whatever we have built there. The losses of a lifetime are too much to resolve or reconcile when we have become old and tired. Their weight will overwhelm our coping mechanisms; they will cannibalize what little energy we have left. As though we've lived too long in the maelstrom of a hurricane, we will become numb and unable to explore the quiet possibilities within.

Feeling our sadness and loss is like suffering the lancing of a wound for draining or the breaking of a bone for resetting. It may be excruciatingly painful, but it's necessary for healing. When we grieve, we feel the sadness of leaving a familiar shore, and then when we are ready, we turn—still sad, but also curious—to face the unknown. This learned skill is crucial to the emotional and spiritual quality of both our current and our last years. Learning how to process our losses keeps us from accumulating grief and makes us expert at recognizing what's happening. By allowing ourselves to grieve, we can learn what supports us while we move through it. Then, when loss and grief visit us again, we already know what we need to stay afloat. With these elements in place we can work through our grief, eventually letting go and moving on.

Because the emotional and physical symptoms of loss and grief (mentioned above) are so debilitating and wide-ranging, our normal ability to function may be impaired when we are dealing with a loss. Periods of "time out" to allow the processing of small losses may be necessary, or we may have to cut ourselves a lot of slack for a year or longer to recover from a massive shattering of the loved and familiar. This is probably not welcome news, but taking it seriously may keep us from adding to our pain through berating ourselves for not being up to par. Allowing ourselves to stay current in our grieving will save us from the awful devastation of having it all crash down on us in our last years.

There are many good books about grieving a major loss but fewer about dealing with the common losses of middle age. For middle-age losses, a good source of support and information is friends who are willing to talk about their own experiences and struggles. In the past few years support groups have begun to form for men and women dealing with the changes of middle age. For the major losses of divorce and death, support groups are offered through counseling centers, hospitals, funeral homes, senior centers, and private psychotherapists.

In my experience, friends and support groups can provide very effective help in healing. Often it seems as though only another person who's going through or has been through a similar loss can really understand what you are feeling. Whether the loss is a small one or a big one, whether your support system is a good friend, a support group, a psychotherapist, or all of the above, it helps to have someone with whom we can speak the truth of our feelings. Sharing what's true for us with people who understand breaks the isolation of sadness and reassures us that we are not crazy, just human. These are also the people most likely to be able to laugh with us over the ironies and absurdities of our changed lives.

When I became co-leader of the local senior center grief

group—the minimum age for joining was fifty—it had already been in existence for three or four years, with people coming and going as they felt the need or desire to be there. Some of those who had started years earlier came back frequently to encourage those who were newly grieving and to share what had helped them get through the really difficult times. Deep friendships, and even two marriages, grew among this group. When a new person came, feeling shattered by his or her loss and confused by the often unhelpful and hurtful reactions of well-meaning but uninformed friends and family, the group would listen carefully, remembering that tears and talking help the most to relieve the awful devastation and isolation of so much pain. A long-term member might tell the group that she also had had a bad week—it would have been their wedding anniversary if her husband had not died. And those who had already survived one or more anniversaries would nod from their firsthand experience of that particular grief. Confidences would begin to flow. Group member Doris reported that she'd had the "week from hell"—nothing had gone right, including locking her keys in her car three times. Then Helen giggled sheepishly as she told us she'd backed her car into the closed garage door twice that month. Hedy told us she'd gone out to lunch earlier in the week wearing her blouse inside out; Mac confessed that he'd paid for his groceries and then walked off without them. What started as knowing chuckles grew to outright laughter as the group shared the pain and absurdity of their erratic, grief-stricken behaviors.

This once-a-month meeting was the best time for many of the participants, who said they could not have survived without it. At the end of the meeting, a restaurant was always chosen where they would go to enjoy a meal, making one night when they wouldn't have to eat alone. On one particular occasion they showed up at the chosen eatery howling with laughter. The delighted host asked them what club or group they were from, and new paroxysms of laughter rocked them when one member replied, "We're a grief group."

Grieving or not, we've got to laugh. Laughter is a twin to tears. Together they are the yin and yang of our love, our recognition of the absurd and of things we care very much about. It's good physical exercise, relieving some of the tension of our impotence in the face of the unfixable. It signifies that although we may be hurting, we are also beginning to accept what we cannot change. Laughter is shared love, support, and the recognition that we're not in the boat alone. It both names and honors our limitations and helps us to remember that the urgent isn't always what's important. Genuine, nonhostile laughter comes straight from the heart and creates an intimacy beyond words. With one exception, I've never conducted a funeral that didn't include laughter.

How wonderful it is, in these mid-to-late middle-aged years of small physical declines, to be with peers who can acknowledge with humor what is happening to us. Even rueful laughter is supportive and healing. And maybe we'll get to be as good at it—humor, that is—as those who've been practicing it for decades, like this eighty-year-old poet, a resident at the retirement community:

## Self Image

Oh, I'm full of pizazz as I sail down the plaza,
 Self-possessed and upbeat as can be,
'Til with shock and rejection, I catch my reflection.
 That dumpy old broad can't be me!

How brutal, how ruthless that moment of truth is!
And to make it most painful of all,
In life's final quarter, how absurd to grow shorter
When inside I'm feeling so tall!

Though three decades past fifty,
I still feel I'm quite nifty.
I have class and I've still got that spark.
I only look harassed because I'm embarrassed
With an image so far off the mark.

What you're hearing discussed is the basic injustice
When looks and true self don't agree.
I ought to look outside the way I feel inside!
How else can you know the real me?

What to do? Be courageous and often outrageous!
Refuse to be put on the shelf!
Take my bows, bless my cheerers
(And avoid full-length mirrors)
Have a ball just being myself!

—Naomi Ridley[7]

Humor can lighten the load our whole lives. I was visiting
two men who shared a room in the retirement facility's nursing home. I'd known them both when they were still living
independently with their wives, who were now deceased.
These men were nearing death themselves. Tom had stopped
talking weeks earlier but could still smile; Merwyn, the more
physically weak of the two, could still carry on a fairly lively
conversation. At the end of the visit I stood up to leave and
said, "Well, I'm on my way out now," and Merwyn responded
lightly, "I hope not the same way we are!"

When you are having to adjust to important changes in your life with the accompanying sadness or grief that is part of the experience, there may be times in which all you need is a whole day in bed with a good book or with the covers over your head. However, if this urge to be in bed lasts a week or more, it's time to consult your physician. You may be slipping into a serious depression that requires medical treatment. Depression is no joke—it can cause chemical and physical changes in the brain and the body. It can depress the immune system and make long-term and even permanent changes in brain chemistry and hormones. Overall, depression can create serious health problems—including death—if it's not treated.

Change in our lives is inevitable. New circumstances will often be accompanied by some degree of grief. Grief is not passive, it's active. It makes us feel our longing for someone or something that has slipped out of our lives forever. It brings us face to face with the fact that we cannot control or possess what we've loved and needed. It creates hollow spaces in the solar plexus and probes them relentlessly, looking for vestiges of what is no more. It leaves us raw and vulnerable. Depending on the magnitude of loss, the sadness can be as minor as a sore tooth or as debilitating as an unanesthetized amputation. Whatever its magnitude, it will never heal if we don't attend to it. Allowing ourselves to feel our sadness and grief is the first and hardest step of caring for ourselves. It's a conscious decision we will probably have to remake many times with any one loss. It takes a lot of self-permission to allow ourselves to have these feelings in a society that demands self-control, is suspicious of strong emotions, and is none too kind with vulnerability. Since we live most of our lives with the illusion of permanence and immortality (even though our rational minds know better), we become very attached to how things are, which makes it very difficult and disorienting to experience the permanent loss of something or someone we've always assumed would be there.

Losses that shatter the heart throw us into feelings we can't control. We fool ourselves if we think we have them in check; we've only repressed them, and they'll catch us off guard eventually. In the meantime, the well of repressed sorrow is expressed in some form of depression, irritability, or bitterness and often as physical symptoms.

Our long-held assumptions about life, about what's fair, and about our place in the world can take an awful beating when an important piece of who we are is permanently removed. Any self-esteem we had that was dependent on these now missing pieces or persons is crushed. This is why it is so important to recognize our experience and take the steps of self-nurture that will help us heal.

Crying is good. Women have known for thousands of years that we feel better after a good cry. The research biochemist Dr. William Frey has proved us right: emotional tears contain chemicals that build up in the body during stress, and when we let go and "cry it out," we are literally releasing some of these stress hormones from our body. Some people have speculated that the inability to express vulnerable emotions, including crying, is a contributing factor in the shorter life spans of men. (The notion that men don't cry is, of course, a sweeping generalization—there are men who weep easily and women who cannot shed tears at all).

Even if we know intellectually that crying is good, sometimes it's hard to let tears out. Many of us, especially men, have been shamed or even punished for crying. Feeling the tears in your throat or behind your face is one thing; getting them out is something else entirely. When you've got grief inside you and the tears just won't come, try crying for some- one or something else that moves you. That's what finally did it for me. I'd been dry-eyed for thirty years, sometimes nearly suffocating on tears that simply wouldn't spill out, even when I tried to force their flow. It wasn't until I worked as a student hospital chaplain that I was finally able to weep—for the dying children, for the dying adults, incredulous that they couldn't do anything to change their fate, and for the exhausted spouses, grandparents, and lovers hovering outside the doors of Intensive Care. I didn't weep copious tears, mind you—old habits are hard to break—but even my small tears of sadness for others were leaking out some of my own sorrow. Now, when a client's situation moves me to tears, I know we are weeping together, for all of us and the tragedy it is some- times to be human.

When change in your life includes loss and you want to weep but cannot do it, another good way to help release tears is to watch a sad movie. Rent the video and watch it at home alone if crying with anyone else around embarrasses you. Or try crying in the shower; somehow the tears seem more anonymous when mixed with water spray and covered by its sound. It's nobody else's business that you cry or how you do it. Remember, not only do tears cleanse the eyes, they are a needed release of stress. If, on the other hand, you simply can- not cry no matter what you try, then experiment with other ways to release the stress of loss, through writing, talking with people you trust, exercise, or whatever else works for you. If you use alcohol for relief, keep in mind that ultimately it's a depressant. It may pick you up for a while, but later it will let you down hard and you'll end up feeling worse than when you started. For many people, using alcohol to cover up painful feelings becomes an addiction. Alcoholism can overtake you before you realize it, especially when you are emotionally vulnerable. Be very careful about using alcohol.

When you are sad and vulnerable, stay out of stressful situations as much as possible. Your emotional tolerance level will be lower than usual if you are processing a loss. If you have a choice of driving on a crowded freeway or taking a pleasant country road to get to the same destination, then build in the extra time for the more pleasant route. If crowds of people play on your nerves harshly, buy your groceries at a small store and save the supermarket or mall for a day when you feel better. Pay attention to the people around you. Whose presence is comforting, and which people leave you feeling exhausted or hurt? The ones in the latter category may be people you love very much, even members of your own family or longtime friends. But while you are vulnerable and hurting, plan to spend time with people whose presence is nurturing, saving the others for those times when you feel stronger.

Discover what is most soothing when you are hurting. It may be having time alone, or perhaps it is spending time with gentle friends who are good listeners and make no demands. If you're feeling lonely but don't have the energy to interact with people, try hanging out in an anonymous crowd for a while—shopping malls are relatively safe places to be with others and alone at the same time. When I'm feeling sad, a walk in the woods or a trip to the zoo or the aquarium does wonders for me. Animals and nature are neutral companions, demanding nothing from me. I've also learned that when I'm numb and dumb with sorrow, colors and textures soothe me. Art galleries and department or fabric stores are good places for me to explore and look and touch with no agenda to buy. I splurge on fresh flowers, I buy comfort foods. I escape through action-adventure movies—the only kind I can concentrate on when feeling numb. And I stand in my shower and weep.

We all have our own ways of coping. When I'm hurting, I'm more likely to go to bed and pull the covers over my head than I am to clean out drawers and closets, but you may find cleaning a release. The point is to learn to recognize when you're experiencing loss and to become familiar with what helps you through it, so that when it comes again you can make these people and these activities or nonactivities part of your agenda at once.

If we stay current in the expression of our sadness and grief, we will be better able to remember that, like the birds who fly into windows, even innocent and perfect creatures get smashed against walls they didn't see. This may help lighten any burden of guilt or denigration we feel over being so vulnerable. When we learn to unburden ourselves of old disappointments and express and release our grief, then we can finally let go of what we cannot keep. Then, in our last stage of life, even with its impairments, limitations, and losses, we can stand solidly on our appreciation of the race we have run and the emotional and spiritual skills we have developed that will help see us through to completion.

The small losses of middle age are the baby steps in learning to cope with the big losses that will eventually come to each of us. Middle age is when we can shift our focus from maintaining an increasingly difficult or irrelevant status quo to adapting creatively to our new circumstances. We can start learning the art of relinquishment in earnest, letting go of what will inevitably slip away despite the intensity of our grasp.

A ninety-four-year-old nursing home resident told me, "I used to be nervous about everything. Now I'm not. This has come with old age. Most of my limitations have brought about a freedom of spirit that has released my mind and heart to explore larger vistas. When I realized recently that I could not remember the poetry I had memorized in youth, it brought an awful pain—but by the next day it didn't matter. Now I live in larger spaces, and the smallest gesture can bring the greatest pleasure." This is not "giving up," nor is it "resignation": it's an intentional, active process that can move us through sorrow to curiosity and interest and pleasure as we see, for the first time, a new and intriguing horizon.

# 3

# You Always
# Make a Difference

A small gesture of kindness made a big difference for me during one of those years I wished would just fall off the calendar. I was three months from earning my college degree, carrying 18 units of classes, going through a very unpleasant divorce, and trying to be a full-time single parent of two children. I had virtually no income. My heart was set on graduate school even before I started college, but now it seemed that there was no way that could happen. One morning, in a fog of despair, I was driving to my classes at the university, unaware of where I was or what I was doing. I pulled into one of the toll booths on the south end of the Golden Gate Bridge and, slowing down but not stopping, stuck my hand out the window palm up, with three quarters for the toll-taker. Whoever was in the booth reached out and gently cupped my hand—a split second of human touch—before efficiently removing the quarters from my palm.

I didn't notice what had happened until I was driving away, and by then I was already too far away to get a look at the toll-taker in my rearview mirror. But that sudden, unexpected human touch turned the lights back on in my head and heart. For days, weeks, and months thereafter I scanned the booths when I crossed the bridge, hoping for a glimpse of someone familiar-looking, wanting and needing to express my gratitude. Twenty years later I still carry that touch in my heart and frequently run on the memory of it. That toll-taker had *seen* me, had maybe even recognized the cloud of despair I was in and then acknowledged the fact that I existed. From that experience I learned that a momentary gesture of kindness can warm a despairing heart, even when it comes from a stranger who does no more than respectfully acknowledge our existence.

There is *never* a time in our lives when we don't make a difference, and we can choose what that difference might be. Integrating this piece of knowledge into our consciousness will remind us to pay attention to how and what we are doing, to be aware of our state of being and the ways in which we affect those around us. If this concept has become an integral part of who we are by the time we reach our last years, we will have the basis for meaning and purpose of our living even if we are ill or disabled.

Independence is a myth of modern American society, a leftover from our pioneer history. The frontier has become cities, parks, recreation areas, and large-scale farming. Rugged individualism now takes the form of men and women climbing the planet's highest mountains, executives bicycling to their offices, or a guy mixing root beer with red wine and liking it. Except for lone survivalists who disappear into the wilderness, few—if any—in technological society are ever really independent. The mountain climbers' lives depend on the skill of their guides and the people who manufacture their equipment; the cycling executives depend on the soundness of their equipment and the courtesy of passing motorists. My friend who mixes root beer with red wine depends on the store to stock both beverages.

The quality and convenience of our modern life depends on others showing up to do their part. Everything we have and do is designed, built, delivered, installed, or serviced by other people. As winter approaches, I am grateful to the road crew who stood under the glaring summer sun on hot asphalt, embedding little orange reflectors down the middle of the unlighted country road that is my route home. Their work has contributed to my safety and extended the number of years I'll be able to drive at night. I am also thankful for all the known and unknown people who laid the technological groundwork that led to the computer chip by which I write these words. You can read this because it was edited, printed, marketed, and distributed by the publisher, a process involving the skill and effort of many people. An optometrist prescribed corrective lenses so you can read. The luxury of reading late into the night is ours because of the inventiveness of Thomas Edison, the skill of people who manufacture our lamps, and the hard work of those who connected our buildings to the utilities system and keep everything operating.

If we pay attention to what goes into everything we have to do, we may begin to notice how odd our assumptions are about our independence. In particular, we may catch sight of our assumption that dependence applies only to the very young, the disabled, and the very old. What we usually think of as our independence—the independence of healthy, strong adults—is actually interdependence.

Self-reliance is possible only because of interdependence with the web of support and services that allow us to make choices and act on them. The quality of each of our days is dependent on who our teachers have been, on farmers, waitresses, secretaries, co-workers, bosses, housekeepers, childcare providers, airline pilots, and bus drivers, as well as the people who make our shoes and our toothpaste and the ones who service our cars. They all make possible our so-called independence. Services and products aren't always perfect, but enough people do their work well enough that we don't even notice that what we're using or doing is possible only because of the creativity, attention, and labor of other human beings.

In the mid-1970s the feminist movement declared "Alice Doesn't Day," encouraging all employed women to stay home from their jobs for one day. Of course very few did—most were employed because they needed the income and couldn't afford to risk losing their jobs. But I was staggered when I pondered the consequences if they *had* stayed home! Without the women who were working in then-invisible positions as secretary, bank teller, file clerk, bookkeeper, waitress, nurse, teacher (the highest positions that most of us could aspire to back then), not even the most powerful CEOs or national leaders could have functioned. It was on Alice Doesn't Day that I first realized that the backbone of this nation isn't made up of the mighty and powerful—the mighty and powerful can function only because they are supported by the skills of ordinary people who show up for work day after day to take care of the details of manufacturing, service, and commerce.

Our political and commercial interdependence has grown to include cooperation between many countries on the planet. My automobile was made in both Japan and the United States; my dinnerware was produced in Italy; my deck is made of boards that may have been cut in Japan from trees grown right here in Oregon. Seen from this perspective, the whole endeavor of life takes on a rather breathtaking cast.

Include in this picture the homeless, the underemployed, and the unemployed, who assist each other as best they can.

We are a massive but functioning choreography. The fact that countless people are involved in everything we do and that things run relatively smoothly speaks to an immense—if unrecognized—global teamwork.

Considering, then, the fact that we're all members of a global team, just how much influence does each of us as an individual have? We look at the mess the world is in and think, "What difference can one person make?" In fact, much of the mayhem in the world is created by one or a handful of individuals. There are innumerable examples of how much damage one person can do. The ethnic hatred aroused by Slobodan Milosevic—whose face is in the media almost every day as I write this book—has been responsible for the murder of innumerable people and has torn Yugoslavia apart. Augusto Pinochet of Chile and Idi Amin of Uganda—to name only two of many—sold their country's natural resources to other nations and pocketed the money while torturing and murdering thousands of their own citizens and starving millions more. (The fact that many of these dictators were trained, put in place, and supported by U.S. tax dollars puts the suffering of their citizens at our doorstep.) The Oklahoma City bomber shattered hundreds of lives and cost taxpayers millions in damages and legal fees. On a slightly smaller scale, think of a gang leader who terrorizes his own neighborhood or an abusive parent whose children will relive the terror of their childhood for their entire lives; a drunk driver whose vehicle is a murder weapon; the surly employee who leaves his coworkers frustrated and exhausted at the end of the day; the sharp-tongued family member who can single-handedly turn a holiday gathering into a nightmare.

Most of us have had some experience with these situations; the injustice and pain make them hard to forget. Looking at the damage one person can inflict is a clue to how much power an individual has, how much of a difference one person can make. If we take a good look beyond the destructive actions of some individuals to see what other people are doing, we will be amazed at and heartened by the goodwill and support that pour forth every day from every quarter of society. I'll give you a few examples.

Operation Nightwatch is a ministry here in Portland that used to pair up volunteers to walk the downtown streets at night and be available for talking or for assistance in obtaining food. One night a Catholic nun and I went out together. From dusk until midnight we went into seedy taverns, ordered coffee, and waited to see if anyone would talk to us. In each place they did, drawn by our clerical garb and curiosity about what we were doing there. In one bar a very thin young woman with too few teeth and too many miles on her face brought her beer over and joined us. She expressed surprise and pleasure at our presence and told us of her current battle with the county. One room on the fourth floor of the old hotel in which she lived was home to an elder who was unable to get around without a wheelchair. The elevators in the hotel had been out of service for weeks, confining him to his room and the toilet down the hall. She and other tenants checked in with him daily, making sure he had what he needed to stay alive. She had begun making two and three visits every week to the county office, first reporting and then reminding the authorities of the plight of her fellow tenant and their landlord's disregard for the local building codes. Her indignation at the injustice to the man propelled her to confront the authorities despite her lack of education, her meager circumstances, and her low social status. She was making a difference by insisting that the authorities enforce the building codes, and she would keep insisting until they did it. That same evening I met an old woman in the lobby of a cheap hotel. Sitting on a dirty couch repaired with duct tape, she was crocheting a lap robe from neon-orange yarn to give to "those poor people in nursing homes." Every month when she got her small Social Security check she went to Newberry's dime store and bought yarn that she lovingly crafted into warm items for people she considered less fortunate than herself.

My night on the streets left me humbled and awed. I'd assumed only bad stuff happened out there. I had never guessed at the respect, caring, and support shared among many of its residents. The walking-the-streets program has been discontinued: as in every metropolitan area, Portland's streets at night have gotten meaner. Operation Nightwatch now maintains a downtown drop-in center that is staffed by volunteers who help people find a place to stay for the night, feed them, and make sure there's a birthday celebration for each regular drop-in. It's the closest thing to home and family that many of their clients have.

Several years ago a group of people who live in downtown Portland's condos and apartments organized a soup kitchen in a park near the center of town. Every Saturday and Sunday afternoon they carry into the park folding tables and food they have bought and prepared themselves to serve hungry homeless and low-income people. The program has become so successful that the church and art museum fronting the park have complained to the city about the large number and type of people it brings to the area. In other parts of town, volunteers haul, split, and deliver firewood to low-income elders who have woodstoves or fireplaces. Portland's naturopathic college provides ongoing medical care at a local drop-in center for homeless kids. Across the nation, volunteers show up every day to prepare and deliver Meals-on-Wheels, while others volunteer to be "senior companions," befriending elders who are homebound and driving them to their doctor's appointments and on other errands. There are many mentoring programs that fill the gaps in some children's lives. Other people volunteer in hospitals to hold and rock drug-addicted babies, soothing their tiny nervous systems with love, touch, and gentle voices. All around the globe, Habitat for Humanity houses are constantly under way, built with donated materials by volunteers who work side by side with the families who will live in them.

Everywhere I go, every place I look, I find people who care about others and actively work to make a difference. In 1984 I traveled to the Middle East and met Arabs and Jews in Jerusalem who had created a day-care center in which their children could grow and play together. These "enemies" wanted their kids to form friendships that might some day make killing each other unthinkable. In the 1980s, during the war against Nicaragua, volunteers from all over the world, including the United States, joined Witness for Peace and traveled to high-risk areas where *contra* soldiers were attacking whole villages and torturing and killing the people in them. The presence of the foreign volunteers, who lived with the peasants in their villages and worked side by side with them in the fields, saved many lives, since killing foreigners was bad public relations for the *contras*. Some of the volunteers were injured and killed anyway, but more came, risking their lives so that others might live. Peace has not yet come to the Middle East, and the conditions the United States pressed on Nicaragua have made life for the peasants nearly impossible.

Life is so desperate for the poor in Nicaragua that where once I could walk on Managua's streets unmolested, now people are mugged in broad daylight. The wealthy have returned, and the poor are poorer than ever. These ongoing problems, however, do not alter the fact that there was joy in working together to make things better. Nor does it erase the ways in which those efforts changed the individuals who were involved in them.

The power one person can have in the life of another is often indescribable. Fifteen-year-old Brandi Wiggins, trapped under the rubble of the Oklahoma City bombing in April 1995, was the last living victim found. Terrified, hurt, and pinned down by piles of heavy rubble, she was given the hope she needed to stay alive by Dr. Rick Nelson, who held her hand and repeated, "I won't let you go, I won't let you go," while others worked to free her. Until her body was uncovered from the rubble, Dr. Nelson could offer only his words of commitment, but I am convinced they were the beacon that kept her alive until she could be removed and receive the medical treatment he could finally provide.

The men and women who work at Engine Company #16 in Chicago are another example of people making a difference. Their station is in the middle of the Chicago Housing Authority's Robert Taylor housing project, the largest—and usually considered the worst—such development in the United States. Ninety percent of the children in the project are fatherless. Well over a decade ago, the fire station opened itself to the community's children. The station staff hold homework classes for students. They repair the kids' bicycles or give them one of the many bikes that have been donated. They collect clothing and shoes for the youngsters and make sure the bathroom facilities are always available to them. Kids come to borrow money, to get help in finding a job, to get a Band-Aid because there's no money for their family to buy any. Often they just come to talk. If a child makes the honor roll at school, these fire personnel go to the school and make a public presentation to the child of a bike, a T-shirt, or some other prize. The firehouse is a sanctuary in the middle of a war zone. Gang members don't attack rivals who show up there, because the fire and paramedic personnel have tended the wounds of members of all the gangs. Staff often come in on their days off to spend time with the children and repair donated bicycles. These are ordinary people doing extraordinary things. There are probably not many ways to measure the effect of these people's commitment to the area's children. Who knows how many of these young people, who live in a society that doesn't appear to believe in them, will find success because these men and women live out the message every day, "You are important to me."

And may we never forget the 1989 image of the unidentified man who stood steady and alone in the face of oncoming military tanks in Beijing's Tiananmen Square. Those who were there say that Chinese soldiers shot him a few blocks from the square after he'd brought the tanks to a standstill. But the image of his straight and unwavering body in the face of such power is burned into the minds and hearts of people all over the world, thanks to the ABC News crew and *Time* magazine, who gave the world this picture of courage.

Individual actions that enhance life in your own neighborhood and workplace accumulate goodwill and improve life on the planet. Although I've used some examples of extraordinary courage and creativity, we don't have to risk life and limb or spend a lot of money to make a difference. It only takes paying attention to ourselves and those around us to extend kindness and, when we are willing, a little time and effort. For example, there are loggers who plant seedlings when they've finished taking the trees from a piece of land; there are countless people who line the streets with their recycling bins filled with materials that will be made into new products; there are people who give blood several times a year. My dentist spends her vacation time volunteering with conservation projects. People choosing simplicity over extravagance in their professional and personal lives free up resources that can be shared with others. The disabled, both young and old, give affection and love that enhance the emotional lives of those who know and assist them. Each of us, always, makes a difference.

That this is so, even when someone has severe physical limitations, was dramatically demonstrated by Ethel, a certified nurse's aide. She fell at work, breaking a hip, and was placed in a nearby nursing home. I went to visit, curious about her experience of being on the receiving end after decades of caring for others. The care was good in this nursing home, she said, and overall she was satisfied with her experience. However, there was one exception—one aide whose shift she dreaded. The young woman was always slow to respond to the call light, and when she finally did come to the door, she would saunter across the room to Ethel's bedside without speaking a word of greeting or asking what was needed. This aide's care was sloppy and often unfinished. She'd assist her patient into the shower but fail to provide a clean gown or change her bed. If a request for fresh water or juice was made, the aide would leave the room wordlessly and often did not return. The shifts this young woman worked were the most difficult experience of Ethel's convalescence.

During one of our conversations Ethel decided she would

make the aide her project. For the next few weeks, whenever that particular aide came to Ethel's door, Ethel greeted her, told her she was glad to see her, and asked how she was. She was warm in her praise of the young woman's small effort. Eventually, feeling accepted, the young aide opened up, and Ethel learned about her difficulties trying to care for three young children single-handedly on a minimum wage. She responded enthusiastically to Ethel's interest in her family, and at Ethel's request she brought in her children's photographs. When I visited three weeks later, Ethel said the change in the aide was dramatic. Now she promptly answered Ethel's call light, arriving at her door with a greeting smile, and she talked with Ethel while she quickly performed and completed the needed care. The payoffs for both women were huge: Ethel no longer dreaded the aide's work shifts because she was now receiving the care she needed. What's more, she had gained an ally in the young woman, and together they shared their experiences and concerns. The young aide had obviously begun to feel better about herself. The change in the quality of her care and her improved attitude enabled her to be hired at a better-paying facility within months after Ethel's discharge. And the two have remained friends.

In our society the assumption is that when we can no longer "do" things we have no quality of life, no purpose, and no contribution to make. But our real significance, at any age and under any circumstance, lies in our "being." "Being" has to do with a quality of presence that is hard to describe. Think about someone you know who feels good to be around, someone you can spend time with and leave feeling energized and good about yourself. This is a person who doesn't have to "do" anything—just being in the same room is a pleasure. Then think of someone you know who leaves you feeling tense, drained, or insecure. It could be someone you love very much, but you find yourself putting off calling them. You approach your time together with resignation, even dread. This person may be well-intentioned, but being with him or her does not shore you up, increase your energy, or make you feel good about yourself. With these people we have to be aware of our own current levels of emotional strength and tolerance before deciding to spend time with them.

A person who is "being" is fully present. They are totally engaged in the moment. This engagement includes an easy appreciation and sense of connection with whomever or whatever they are relating to at the time. These people are aware of a job well done or a difficulty surmounted and will respect and often acknowledge the person who has accomplished it. "Being" is a state of heart and mind that is receptive and able to listen carefully.

We all need appreciation, no matter who we are. Listening and acknowledging someone nonjudgmentally is an extremely important part of this exchange, and all of us can do that for each other.

"Being" is important in any relationship. When we are old and may find ourselves needing assistance, both the provider and the receiver have "being" to offer the other. This offering of genuine presence can make a world of difference, as we saw in the relationship between Ethel and her young aide.

No matter what our circumstances may be, our presence and our choices make a difference—whether good or bad— to the totality of the life we share. If you are a parent, you can give your children love, respect, and guidance that will build a foundation of self-worth, values, and confidence for the rest of their lives. In doing so, you give to the world the priceless gift of emotionally healthy and values-based human beings.

If you and your partner create safety for each other through acceptance and commitment, you will build an emotional foundation from which each of you can go out to the world with confidence and security. If we are cooperative at work, we will make everyone's day more pleasant and productive. Even if we're flat on our back in bed, we can still—as Ethel did—acknowledge the presence of those caring for us in a way that helps them know they matter. On the other hand, if we're irritable and hard to please, we can make life miserable for everyone around us.

The effect of a small gesture is not something that can be measured precisely. How can one register the impact of a genuine smile or greeting? Imagine that a warm greeting makes the grocery clerk's feet ache a little less for a moment or two, enabling her to smile at her next customer, who, when he returns to his car is more patient waiting for the older woman to cross the street, who, appreciating the driver's patience, smiles at the little girl playing on the sidewalk. Having received that smile, the little girl feels important, so when she goes home she hugs her tired mom, who is so touched by this show of affection that she pets the dog instead of kicking it, which makes the dog so happy that he kisses the little girl. Now the little girl is feeling so good from the older woman's smile, her mom's hug, and the dog's happy slurp that she goes outside and unexpectedly shares her bike with the boy next door. He is so surprised and pleased by this unusual turn of events that he generously plays with the funny-looking kid who just moved into the neighborhood. The new kid is so relieved to have made a friend that he goes home smiling and happy. This relieves his worried parents, and so when the boy's mother goes to the grocery store, she is feeling more optimistic about the new neighborhood, so she smiles and greets the grocery clerk whose feet had been hurting . . .

Let's not forget the practice explored in the chapter "Befriending Yourself," that's foundational to how we work, play, and respond to the life around us: that of being our own friend. The Christian Bible's great commandment includes loving your neighbor as yourself. Within that instruction is contained the idea that we cannot know and love our neighbor unless we know and love ourselves. When we are ignorant of and abusive to ourselves, being genuinely accepting and hospitable to others may be difficult and take too much out of us. If we are not aware of what drives our behavior, then we won't have the ability to make choices based on our best values. Instead, decisions will be based on obligation, fear, resentment, greed, or self-importance, all of which carry destructive consequences. What's more, people who are the recipients of this contaminated attention know it on some level. They feel diminished or used and objectified. For those of us who are limited by self-ignorance, it is nearly impossible to forgive others' mistakes because we can't forgive our own. Unable to understand our own feelings and behaviors, we will never be accurate in our discernment of other people's. It's difficult to genuinely empathize with anyone when we cannot empathize with ourselves. Knowing, loving, and respecting ourselves is our responsibility to the web of interdependence that supports us all.

Whether your relationships are good or bad, they will make a big difference in how you will experience your last years. In the preceding chapter, "Learning to Grieve," I spoke of Eleanor, who died separated from her family because of a decision she'd made about her daughter-in-law fifty years earlier. In the chapter "Befriending Yourself," Valerie's interactions with her daughter were so upsetting that her daughter had left the state to get away from her, and now that they lived near each other again, Valerie still did not know how to communicate anything but disapproval. Both Eleanor and Valerie, clinging to their judgments, felt abandoned and lonely in the last years of their lives. Their deaths ended any possibility of reconciliation with their families. For their children and grandchildren this was an irretrievable loss.

I like the story I once heard about an older woman who began inviting, one by one, her relatives and friends to tea. Before she died or became impaired, and while she was still clear-headed and able, she wanted to tell each of them the specific ways he or she had graced her life. She told them what she loved and admired about them and shared her hopes for their future. Her acceptance of the naturalness of her aging and death put her guests at ease, giving them the opportunity to express their feelings too and to receive her love and blessing with open hearts. The old woman lived several more years, but having openly discussed the inevitable fact of her demise had liberated them all from the pretense that nothing was changing. Once she had expressed to them, and they to her, the important things that needed to be said, her friends and family were free to relate with her in the moment, confident of their importance to her and hers to them. Her death, when it came, left a hole in their lives, but one that was filled with the love, respect, and hope she had given them. Her last years were a benediction to the lives of those who cared for her and to the family and friends who survived her.

Providing care for an elder who needs assistance is hard work. It is both physically and emotionally demanding. The best caregivers are those who are acutely aware and respectful of the vulnerability of their patient. They also sense, on some level, the sacred nature of living and working on this threshold between life and death. Their care is efficient and their presence is healing—they understand that *receiving* care is hard work too. The people they assist feel valued and important. Some caregivers leave the job after a while because the accumulated grief brought about by the deaths of the many people they've become attached to becomes too much to bear. Others stay, knowing that grieving is part of the work, a price they are willing and able to pay.

I have been told by some grown children that one of their greatest joys was the privilege of caring for an ill and dying parent—a chance to give back something of what they had received from their mother or father. It's wonderful when an elder can be cared for by a loving relative or friend. That is not always possible, of course, but fortunately a hired care provider can often establish a respectful and even loving relationship with a client. The care provider's job is to give needed assistance courteously and efficiently. The client's job is to receive the assistance courteously and as efficiently as he or she is able to. Within this framework, the human interaction—if it includes mutual respect and especially affection—can be a life-enhancing experience for both. For people with histories devoid of love, whether they are providing care or receiving it, this may be their best experience of respect and affection. But the relationship can also be very destructive if denigration, neglect, or any kind of abuse is inflicted. We tend to worry about caregivers being abusive, but it works both ways: I have seen nurse's aides reduced to tears and their stress elevated to unbearably high levels by patients who are mean or even cruel to them.

A nursing home resident in her nineties whom I worked with was faced with a stark choice. She had survived a serious illness that she was sure would finally allow her to die. At her request, no extraordinary life-preserving measures had been taken—she had made it clear to all of us that she did not want to be kept alive. But she didn't die; she recovered. All indications were that she could live for several more years. She was walking again with assistance, but she was furious that she was still alive. She harbored a fierce bitterness for several weeks until she realized, upon awaking one morning, that she had a choice—she could remain bitter for the rest of her days, making herself and those around her miserable, or she could accept what was happening and give up her anger, which might make life more pleasant for herself and for those who associated with her. She chose what she knew, given her values and experience, was her only viable option—acceptance of her situation. For weeks she continued to struggle with her anger, as she grieved the loss of her death, but over time her emotions aligned with her decision to accept her circumstances.

It was only days before she realized that acceptance of her lot was not enough to provide meaning in her daily life. So she upped the ante—she decided to do whatever was in her power to make those who were caring for her feel good about themselves. This became her daily purpose. It wasn't easy. She told me that for weeks she had to struggle in the morning to remember what she'd decided and then decide it again. Every morning she had to push herself emotionally to rise above her disappointment at finding herself still among the living. But each week, she said, it became easier. She'd begun to derive genuine pleasure from seeing the difference her encouragement made to those who cared for her. A few months later she had the revelation that the energy of encouragement she was giving to the staff was not confined to her heart or her room or even the nursing home in which she resided, but that it extended out to all of life. She still longed for death, but at the same time she felt strongly that she was contributing to the good of the world.

One of the many parts of my job that I cherished was meeting with nursing home staff. The housekeepers, nurse's aides, licensed practical nurses, registered nurses, and sometimes members of the administration gathered to talk, not about the patients, but about the issues that were personally important in our work. I was constantly impressed with the quality of the relationships these people had with their patients and their commitment to the physical and emotional well-being of those in their care. Their commitment showed up not only in their assigned tasks but also in the myriad ways they went the extra mile for their patients' comfort and pleasure. There was the housekeeper who loaned her cassette player and tapes to a blind resident who loved classical music, nurse's aides who came in on their days off with small gifts for their patients' birthdays, others who came in on their days off to bring their pets or their children to visit. And there were exhausted nurses and aides who stayed on when their shifts ended to sit at the bedside of someone who would otherwise die alone.

I wondered why these people chose these difficult nursing home jobs in the first place and why they then extended themselves even further. During a series of classes I taught shortly after I'd begun work there, I asked them, "Why do you do this work? What makes it okay to come back day after day to do something most of the rest of the world is avoiding?" Their responses revealed instance after instance of caring between staff member and patient. "When a resident tells me she likes my hairdo"; "when he tells me to drive home safely but to hurry back"; "when she squeezes my hand";

"when he smiles at me"; "when we share hugs and kisses"—
these were the moments, they said, that made their work
worthwhile. A housekeeper said that a resident's comment
"I've missed you," was a dose of medicine she really needed.
An aide responded, "I need my patients' love and caring to
make my life complete." Another housekeeper said, "When I
tell a resident I'm leaving and say 'I'll see you,' having them
respond 'I hope so' really means a lot." These people work
because they need the income, but they do *this* work because
they receive love, caring, and respect from their patients.

I think of one resident whose being lightened all who
came in contact with her. She and her husband had moved
into the nursing home because her husband, who had cared
for her since a stroke years earlier had left her right side paralyzed, was dying of cancer. Shortly after their arrival, he died.
In a period of a few weeks this disabled woman had lost her
husband, her home, and her routines. Her grief was profound, but she did not withdraw or become bitter. Instead,
she was interested in the people around her, both staff members and other residents. When she was outfitted with a
motorized wheelchair she ventured farther out into the facility complex. Eventually she became so proficient at self-care
that she moved from the nursing home to an apartment in
another part of the retirement community. While she continued to grieve the loss of her beloved husband and home, she
was still able to listen with genuine interest to other people's
stories. Everywhere she went on campus, her interest and
great sense of humor endeared her to other people. She was
severely handicapped physically, but it was not possible to be
in the same room with her without feeling affirmed in one's
own humanity. Hers was a presence that comforted and
healed even as she grieved her many losses.

On the other hand, I once knew a young, high-powered executive who said the world was full of jerks. Then he went into psychotherapy to try to learn how to deal with his frustrations and to save his marriage. After some time in this process, he was shocked to discover that the jerk was none other than himself! The people—including his wife—whom he had disparaged were merely responding to his assumption of superiority over them and his unreasonable expectations and demands.

We all have choices to make about the quality of our presence and how we will affect those around us. The quality of our presence is dependent not on what we can or cannot "do" but on the essence of who we are and how we relate to others. Becoming the presence we would like to be is an intentional work. It grows while we make peace with ourselves and with life.

Gestures of kindness, courage, honesty, and love tend to be small and quiet, and most of them are made by ordinary human beings. But these acts create and sustain a dense web of commitment that holds this planet and its people together. The web is so resilient that it will never be completely destroyed, because it is constructed of human goodwill rather than bricks, money, or nationalism. Even in those places where the web is severely damaged by war and other outrages, there are still the small acts of kindness and encouragement that can make the difference between hope and despair, life and death.

We are all part of this web, standing side by side in the same large circle. We are members of the same species, holding hands with the living and with the dead, whose legacies have helped shape our current lives. We pass our love and our disappointments through our work, our hands, and our eyes.

Many of us stand with faces downcast, afraid to see the love and beauty of those around us and how profoundly we are connected. We are also afraid of seeing the love and dazzling beauty within ourselves. We stumble along doing the best we can. We mess up, we don't live up, we fall down and pick ourselves up again, we love and we die. But no matter what, we are connected. We make a difference, each one of us, no matter how sick, how frail, how old we are.

Becoming aware of how extraordinarily interdependent we are expands our minds and hearts to perceive the larger vista of life and our place in it. We can begin to see that we are not solitary figures in the world but part of the huge web that holds it all together. With this awareness we will also recognize that our choices maintain, strengthen, or weaken the integrity of the whole.

Awareness of our interdependence makes possible the experience of gratitude of the heart, which is far more profound than the polite "thank you" of the mind. The heart's experience of gratitude provides the foundation for all joy and love.

No matter what your circumstances, you will always have a gift for others. The expression of love does not require mobility, vision, hearing, great intelligence, or even speech. If we can breathe, we can love. I believe love *is* our work and that it is not finished until our last breath. Maybe, after all, that's what this last stage of life is about—our becoming what the ancient Hebrews called *Ruach*—the breath of God.

# 4

# Losing the Mind,
# Finding the Heart

*Experiences of Alzheimer's Disease*

My week had been filled with clients suffering loss: the loss of a spouse, child, sibling, or best friend, of health, of home or car, of vision, movement, or hearing. By Thursday afternoon my tolerance level for my own impotence in the face of so much that was unfixable had dropped to zero. I needed something to nurture my battered spirits. I walked over to the nursing home to visit Maisy and was delighted to find her in her room. Alzheimer's disease had transformed Maisy into a childlike elder whose words made so little sense that they couldn't distract anyone from her sunny disposition. She invited me in for an invisible cup of tea and offered me an invisible plate of cookies. Like kids playing house, we ate and drank and carried on a nearly incomprehensible dialogue. I listened for the feelings behind her garbled speech for cues to holding up my end of the conversation.

After our tea and cookies she began to clean up, and I insisted on helping her. We sat side by side on her bed, laughing and giggling, washing and drying imaginary dishes, me with the heartfelt hope that no staff members would walk by the open door and observe us. How could I explain to them that this was not silliness, it was a sacred exchange? I had offered her companionship on her own terms, and by helping me step outside of the heavy realities I'd been working with, she had instilled new life in me. Whenever I needed a boost, I visited Maisy.

A national survey conducted in 1996 by the Alliance of Aging Research showed that the second-greatest fear connected with growing old in the United States is developing Alzheimer's disease. The number-one fear is living in a nursing home. Death came out in lowly sixth place, behind losing physical attractiveness (fifth), being lonely (fourth), and becoming a financial burden (third).

There are more than one hundred identified forms of dementia—impairments of the brain—of which Alzheimer's disease (AD) is the most common, occurring in 56 percent of the cases of dementia. Some of the dementias are curable, but Alzheimer's, so far, is not. More than four million people in the United States are currently diagnosed with Alzheimer's, and unless a cure is found, fourteen million are projected to be diagnosed with it by the middle of the twenty-first century.[8] Since Alzheimer's disease was shown in the survey to be one of the most feared aspects of aging, I decided it needed its own chapter. As of this writing, 47 percent of people over age eighty-five have Alzheimer's disease. If it's in the future for nearly half of us who live that long, we need to look at AD in a way that helps us understand the experience of the person diagnosed with it. I have put this chapter in the "Emotional Preparation" part of the book because there is some evidence that doing the emotional work of preparation for late life may also improve our quality of life should we one day have Alzheimer's or one of the other dementias.

The disabilities and illnesses of late life require the patient to do most of the work of accommodating or relearning, as in walking or talking after a stroke. With Alzheimer's disease it is the family and friends who have to make the major adaptations.

For the people closest to the one with Alzheimer's, this adjustment is profoundly complicated by the fact that they have known this person and his or her competencies for decades. To those who watch someone they have known and loved being permanently altered by the progression of Alzheimer's, the disease is an unmitigated horror. Watching your wife mistake the telephone for the radio, wondering why none of the buttons turn it on, is heartbreaking; having your husband of fifty years forget who you are and refuse to sleep in the same bed with "that strange woman" leaves you feeling helpless and rejected. When a friend who has spoken to audiences all over the nation suddenly produces sentences that make no sense at all, we don't know how to respond to her. For those who have known these people intimately, what response could there be to the changes inflicted by Alzheimer's except helplessness, rage, and grief? Every new behavior and/or personality change stands in stark contrast to how he or she used to be. And each time we remember who this person was and what he or she could do before the disease, we are hit again by grief and a profound sense of how unfair life can be.

Once past the initial stages of AD, during which the person who has the disease may be aware of the changes occurring, he or she moves into a different time frame. The afflicted person lives in the moment. Past and future become more abstract and difficult to consider cognitively, until the ability to consider them disappears forever. Meanwhile, the caregiver's life is turned upside down with nothing but the unpredictable and bizarre to count on. Then the work and adjustment to this disease is all on the shoulders of family and friends. They are being challenged to accept and to see with new eyes a person they've counted on and grown used to over many years. They are being asked to acquire an unusual level of patience, sensitivity, and attention so they can discern the reasons behind their loved one's new and unfamiliar behavior. This is a level of attention that may never have been required of them before. Caregivers who are struggling to live with these radical and heartbreaking changes carry understandably huge loads of rage and grief. It is usually from their perspective that we hear the most about Alzheimer's disease.

Reconciliation to the changes Alzheimer's imposes on others is hard, often downright impossible for those who knew them most deeply before they were stricken. But if we can't let go of who they were, we cannot see who they are now. Professionals and volunteers who provide companionship and "hands-on" care to the Alzheimer's-afflicted often observe that in the long run the disease is harder on the family than on the patient.

I want to present the experience of Alzheimer's from my perspective, a perspective acquired by working intimately with AD people without being burdened by the assumptions and expectations of a long, shared personal history. I want to show you who some of them are in the moments of their daily lives. Because we are so afraid of this disease, I want to show that even if we "lose our mind" we don't lose our humanity. For many people with Alzheimer's, a satisfying and meaningful quality of life is still possible. The best way I know to illustrate this is through the stories of people I have known.

## Harold

When I'd passed the nurses' station earlier, Harold was in his usual place. He sat on a corner of a nurse's desk in the middle of ringing phones, paperwork, social workers, an occasional nurse's aide, and the case manager. Because the Alzheimer's-stricken Harold was a gentle, loving presence who made everyone feel more relaxed, the staff welcomed him into their already cramped quarters. In acknowledgment of his decades as a successful businessman and employer, they often expressed to him their appreciation for his "help."

When I returned to the nurses' station sometime later, he'd grown tired of the bustle and was leaving. His slow Alzheimer's shuffle had gotten him to the doorway just as I arrived to go in. We stood face to face as he reached out and began to fondle the buttons on my blouse. I held my breath, wondering what his next move would be. His fingers wandered to my name tag and glided back and forth over the smooth plastic that displayed my photo and title. Then he cupped his hand and, raising it to my cheek, tenderly held my face. We looked into each other's eyes. In that moment, all externals disappeared in deference to human connection. No words were spoken—Harold had few he could form anymore. But something deep, beyond words, passed between us.

Except for having Alzheimer's, including the shuffling walk typical of the disease, Harold was physically healthy. He freely wandered the corridors and public areas of his floor. His emotional life was rich with human connection that flowed out to those around him. He was interested in everyone and everything, and in the time his attention span allowed, he would stop and take in whatever or whomever he saw, as a new and holy thing. When he was angry—usually about being showered and dressed—he expressed his irritation by physically lashing out. But no one was harmed; the staff were skilled at diverting anger. He had his bad days—as we all do—in which he expressed irritation or sadness, but they were few. Most days he was loving and happy. In the end, death came quickly for Harold. Up and shuffling about one day, he was confined to bed with pneumonia the next. His life ended a short two weeks later.

The mentally impaired Harold lived his last years as if every space, every moment, was sacred. Anyone entering his presence felt quieter and more calm, the better to receive his gentleness. This man, to the very end, gifted all who came near.

## Faith and Carl

I met Faith in an early stage of her Alzheimer's, when she and her husband, Carl, carried on a more or less "normal" life in their apartment in the retirement community. She could still hold a mostly coherent conversation. She dozed a lot—so often, in fact, that my visits often entailed my sitting or lying next to her on their king-size bed. We would talk about her life and giggle at the absurdity of things in general. She had a great sense of humor.

Over the next couple of years, things worsened for both her and Carl as her mind slipped further away. She grew increasingly dependent on Carl to dress and toilet her. There were stretches of time when she was hostile, times when she physically fought him as he tried to help her. There were awful periods when she would pace the floor, wringing her hands and weeping, unable to articulate the source of her distress.

It was becoming hell for both of them, and the professionals involved were not always helpful. Her psychiatrist was uninterested, the family physician said that there was nothing more to do, the social services staff felt that Faith should be in the nursing home. All were convinced that the toll on Carl of caring for her was too high. It *was* high. His own arthritic pain pushed him to the limit of his tolerance; her erratic behavior and moods pushed him past that. He lost his temper and yelled at her; he even "strong-armed" her once in a while—actions he confessed to me with shame and remorse.

Carl pleaded with the doctors for more information and alternative treatments. They said he was unrealistic, in denial, and they recommended that he undergo a psychiatric evaluation, which he refused to do. They didn't understand that he couldn't accept the loss of his life's partner while leaving even one stone unturned.

Carl started keeping a diary in which he noted, hour by hour, Faith's behaviors and mood changes. He recorded the effects of her various mood-related medications. With this information he began to see which behaviors seemed directly brought on by her medications. On his own, he started to carefully adjust her dosages according to the information he had gathered in his recorded observations. Every day was trial and error, but eventually her mood swings leveled out. Gone were the combativeness, the depression, the awful hours of hand-wringing and uncontrollable weeping.

The fact that Carl made his own decisions about how much medication to give Faith, and when, would make most physicians shudder in horror. In any case, the medical staff who were working with this couple had already made up their minds: Faith should be living in a nursing home, and Carl's inability to accept this meant that something was terribly wrong with him. These conclusions were based on a twenty-minute appointment every one to three months and the occasional appointment they were given with the psychiatrist who was responsible for prescribing Faith's mood-altering medications. The psychiatrist refused to engage in discussion with Carl, who always accompanied Faith at these sessions; in fact, he showed little interest in either of them. The "experts," having made up their minds, weren't listening.

Carl's taking control of Faith's medication was a move that should not normally be undertaken. If you have a receptive physician who works with you as a team, one who listens to your input, responds accordingly, and is available when changes occur, you're probably in good hands. In this case, though, Carl's level-headedness and insight in the face of closed-minded and uninterested physicians resulted in better care for Faith.

Faith had a need to be moving when she wasn't taking one of her many naps, so, arm in arm, she and Carl walked miles every day up and down the corridors of every floor of the retirement facility. Occasionally she surprised him with complete sentences, but mostly the few words she spoke were incoherent.

Slowly her physical capacities diminished. She forgot how to get in and out of the car, forgot how to stand up or sit down, did not know what to do when faced with stairs. Carl gently guided her around obstacles, helped her stand, sit, and walk, and spent hours sitting in the living room with her while she dozed in her chair.

Faith's disease had profoundly changed both of them. Every night Carl thanked God that he had her with him this additional day, and every night he held her tenderly. In the years of hard work it took to accept her limitations and decline, he had also learned to see her in the moment, to catch the spark of humor and recognition that still visited her eyes and face from time to time. They had walked through hell together, and in the process he had learned a different kind of love—a bond unsullied by words and favors, but fed by the nonverbal power that passed between them. Those times that her eyes sought his, carrying to him her mute love, he saw, received, and reciprocated. Along with his grief and fatigue, Carl discovered levels of patience and compassion unknown to him before, and an inner peace more profound than he had imagined possible.

Three years after the medical staff insisted that Faith needed to be in the nursing home, she finally had to go. Her physical care had become more than Carl's arthritic body could handle. But every morning he arrived at her room in the nursing home after she was dressed and fed, and he pushed her in her wheelchair back to their apartment. He took her to the dining room for morning coffee and for lunch. She couldn't talk anymore; she moved hardly at all, looking neither right nor left. But sometimes she smiled, even occasionally convulsed with an inner chuckle. And when she made eye contact with Carl, a wave of unspeakable love passed between them.

Carl was not grateful to Alzheimer's for the peace and love he grew to experience with Faith. But he admitted that Alzheimer's was what caused his relationship to life, and to Faith, to grow in this new way. Their long marriage as they knew it no longer existed, but he said their love was deeper and stronger than it had ever been.

To see the "who" that is left in the Alzheimer-damaged person, we must leave our world and enter hers. Carl learned after a couple of years of much trial and error not to correct Faith's erratic behavior but to listen and respond to the feelings he discerned behind it.

## *Betty*

Betty had gone into a nursing home because her safety requirements had moved beyond what her husband, himself disabled, could physically provide. Healthy aside from her Alzheimer's, she was restless, physically strong, and territorial. Unfortunately, her need for both safety and freedom of movement could not be met in a nursing home designed to accommodate the very ill and frail. The nursing staff's constant activity and noise overstimulated Betty and increased her restlessness. The combination of her restlessness and territoriality took her into the rooms of other, more frail residents. She frightened them with demands that they leave, or blocked their doors so they couldn't get out. The medication that relieved her restlessness caused her to be unsteady on her feet. Fearing that she would fall and injure herself, the staff recommended that Betty be moved to a facility more appropriate to her needs.

Betty's new residence, not a nursing home, is designed to accommodate the physically healthy and active Alzheimer's client. She shares a room that opens directly onto a large public area furnished like a living room, with wall-to-wall carpeting, comfortable seating for conversation, and a kitchen and dining area at the L-shaped end. The noise and activity levels are kept very low, lessening the need for medication to control the restlessness and agitation caused by overstimulation. In this calmer setting, with fewer medications necessary, Betty's walking is now stable and her chances of falling greatly diminished. If she sleeps during the day and wanders all night, that's okay too—doors to the elevators are secured so she can't wander off her floor and out of the building. The small, cozy kitchen is open twenty-four hours a day, seven days a week, with snacks and beverages always available and a staff person on hand for quiet conversation and company.

When I went to visit Betty at her new home a few weeks after her move, I was astonished at the change in her. She sat with four other men and women watching a 1940s movie on a small television set whose volume was turned low. Gone was the pinched, angry look on her face. She smiled calmly and took the hand her husband offered. She recognized him and seemed to recognize me. I introduced myself to the others in the group, each of whom responded with a handshake and their own name. One of them, a beautiful woman wearing a black turtleneck sweater, her gorgeous white hair in a French roll with loose wisps haloing her face, introduced herself happily as Alice. Then, throwing her arms wide, she gaily declared, "Alice in Wonderland!" When Betty was asked later if she knew where she was, she replied with a big smile, "A resort!"

Alice and Betty, both with Alzheimer's disease, are happy women. They are in a setting designed to accommodate their strengths and their impairments. Betty, once angry and bullying because she could not cope with the routines of a medical setting (a level of care she didn't yet require), now feels she is living in a resort, with things to do and people to be with.

One woman with Alzheimer's, in a lucid moment during the early stages of her dementia, told me that relationships were the most important thing to her, especially people's reaction to her. She said she was interested and stimulated by them. She added, "As long as I can move around and have a little fun, I'm grateful I can't remember everything."

## *Helene*

Helene had late-stage Alzheimer's and could no longer speak words, although she still smiled for those who came near and made eye contact. She shared a room in a nursing home with her lifetime friend Rosalie, who had severely disabling osteoporosis but not dementia. I visited them weekly. While her roommate Rosalie and I talked, Helene made "huh-huh-huh" noises next to us. Rosalie told me it nearly broke her heart, listening to the sounds that Helene made most of the day and night. "I remember what she used to be like, and now just listen to that," Rosalie said. "It's so awful I just wish she could die!" For a while we listened in silence to the sounds Helene was making. They were soft and repetitive. When the nurse's aide came in to get Helene up and take her out for a walk, her sounds became distressed, rising in pitch and coming closer together. Here was something new and strange and therefore frightening. It was part of her daily routine, but she couldn't remember that. The kindness of the nurse's aide reassured Helene, however, and by the time she was seated in her wheelchair the huh-huh-huhing had changed to chuckling sounds.

During my visit the next week Rosalie and I listened some more. When Rosalie and I laughed, Helen's huh-huh-huhs changed to chuckling sounds; when we talked, the huh-huh-huhs moved softly up and down a few notes—a song of participation. I mentioned to Rosalie that repetitive movements and sounds are often used for self-comfort and calming by those who cannot do it in other ways. "You knew her as an officer in World War II, when she was strong and assertive," I pointed out to Rosalie. "Listen to who she is now, comforting herself with the sound of her voice, reassuring herself that she still is, and at the same time participating in our conversation."

Rosalie had to work at seeing Helene's noises in such a positive way; in her mind she still related to the mentally intact and extremely competent Helene. But she told me the next week that in listening to Helene's vocalizations she realized that they indicated distress only when something new—and unremembered—was happening. As soon as Helene was reassured that she was safe and cared for, Rosalie noted, the sounds of distress changed to expressions of pleasure or comfort.

It's hard to see an old friend in a new light. Given our thinking minds and all the assumptions we have about what's dignified and acceptable, it's hard to adjust to the new situation, understand the subtleties of our friend's behavior, and assess her quality of life accurately. We tend to see new behavior as bizarre and distressing when in fact it may be quite meaningful.

## Abigail and Henry

It would not be fair of me to imply by these anecdotes—all of which are true—that all those stricken with Alzheimer's have a high quality of life. Sometimes they can still tell us how they are feeling, but when they lose that ability, we have only their body language to help us discern what their experience may be. Some can lie in a vegetative state for months on end with no response to stimuli. How can we know if they can hear us or have feelings anymore?

In Abigail's case, it appears to those of us around her that a vegetative state would have been a blessing. While her devoted husband was living, he spent many hours with her every day in the nursing home. His worst nightmare, because she had no one else, was that he would die before she did. A fast-moving, lethal cancer made his nightmare a reality.

Abigail had always been extremely restless in the nursing home, unable to stay still except at those times when her husband was with her. Now, with his permanent absence, her agitation grew worse. She couldn't walk or talk but was otherwise physically strong and relatively young and healthy—in other words, she would probably outlive her husband by many years. Every day the staff exercised her, dressed her, and put her in a chair in the public area. She had to be restrained in the chair because she threw herself about so violently that she would have hurt herself otherwise. She vocalized—sometimes whimpering sounds, sometimes sounds that we could only deduce were related to pain. Although no source for physical pain could be found, she had plenty of reasons to be grieving. Everyone felt bad for her. Seeing her restrained and struggling all day long, we all carried grief in our hearts for her, but there was nothing more that anyone could think of to be done to ease what appeared to be terrible and consistent suffering. As of this writing, Abigail is still alive.

Henry's story is a painful one also. When I first met him and his wife of more than fifty years, he was already in a vegetative state. He had once been a well-known and -loved law professor. His wife was very proud of him and introduced him to me as if he could smile and respond. If there was any cognitive part of his brain still functioning, it was not apparent. He lived in this condition for over two years, with no machines or heroic measures taken to keep him alive.

I have included both Abigail and Henry here because I don't want to mislead you into thinking that Alzheimer's is never devastating to the patient. Even the best of care does not always ensure a good quality of life. But I do want to impress upon you that not everyone with Alzheimer's has a nightmarish experience like Abigail's or a long vegetative span like Henry's.

## Ursula

Ursula's background was nursing. When the impairments of Alzheimer's disease required her to move to a nursing home, she simply picked up on what she knew best. Unable to form words, she pushed her wheelchair from room to room, smoothing the sheets and blankets on residents' beds, feeling foreheads and pulses, making soothing sounds, plumping pillows. While there were some residents who experienced her comings and goings as an intrusion and complained—the staff steered Ursula away from those rooms whenever possible—others looked forward to her visits, eager recipients of her tender attentions. Ursula was happy in the familiarity of a medical setting in which she could provide service. Had her activity not been understood by the staff and recognized as an expression of her caring and self-identity, she might not have been allowed the ministrations that brought meaning to her days and comforted those who received her attentions.

## Lester

Sue Silvermarie, a social worker and poet who works with people with Alzheimer's, wrote about Lester, with clues to how his history determined his current behavior:

### The Gentleman

A small and meticulous man,
he walks fast, talks fast,
coughs like an elephant,
and routinely asks with a hopeful smile,

Do you like me?
Lester goes back to bed several times a day
and draws the spread over his head.
When he's up and about he always wears a suitcoat.
He used to have a lot of money.

On this unit residents can't keep cash.
When Lester lived on the first floor,
he could withdraw $10 a week
and spend it in the vending machines.
No such freedoms now, to spend,
to leave the floor, be responsible.
I told him when he came,
he'd have to turn over his cash.
Reluctantly he complied,
all but a single dollar bill
in a wallet under his pillow.

Today his confused roommate
lay down on the wrong bed.
Lester picked up a cane
and beat him unconscious.
The heavyweight aide who walked in on the scene
could barely halt
the small man in a violent trance.
Lester the gentleman is incensed
that we suspect him of such an act.
He denies beating his roommate
who required thirteen stitches.
He does recall
being unable to get to his wallet."9

How much of the bizarre behavior of the person with Alzheimer's disease is due to biological impairment and how much to his or her life history is hard to know, but many experts in the field believe that such behaviors are meaningful and can be traced to earlier events. It may also be a way in which people resolve the unfinished business of their lives.[10]

## Frederick

Frederick, a tall, soft-spoken, well-educated man, had been a talented artist until Alzheimer's destroyed his ability to use the tools of his art. His care requirements became greater than his wife could provide, so reluctantly she admitted him to a nursing home, where he soon became a favorite of staff and residents. Always gracious and cooperative, Frederick was plagued by one horror: he could see a terrifying abyss—a bottomless pit—in the corner of his room. The staff moved him to another room, but the abyss was there as well. Every room they tried eventually included the abyss—only the public areas were safe. The far left corner of his room, the space that held the abyss, was finally blocked off by various pieces of furniture so he could not accidentally fall in. Some days, in his mind, the hole was not there, and he was able to relax in his room and sleep through the night. On the days it loomed large and threatening, he paced restlessly in the public areas until the community activities quieted him.

Was Frederick's abyss created by an old, unacknowledged terror, from perhaps as early as childhood? Or was it simply caused by the misfiring of a damaged brain? We don't have ways to know that yet. But in the decade since Frederick died, extensive research has produced new medications that often help control hallucinations and support higher functioning.

We'll never know now for sure, but it's possible that if these chemicals had been available to Frederick, his abyss would not have existed.

## Sheila

A large black-and-white portrait of Sheila hanging on the wall over her nursing home bed could have been of Eleanor Roosevelt, so tall and dignified did she stand between the Doric columns of the university library she once directed. Now gaunt and stooped, she was unrecognizable as the woman in the portrait.

Sheila, who had never married, had moved to the retirement facility two decades earlier and had chaired many of the program committees steering the cultural, educational, and social life of the community. With the first signs of her dementia she began to withdraw from these activities, eventually becoming reclusive. When her memory impairment prevented her from remembering meals and medications, she moved to the nursing home. As her mind slipped further and further away, this once intimidating woman—she had been listed in *Who's Who in America*—became childlike, interacting freely and happily with all who came in contact with her.

Eventually Sheila lost the ability to walk. Although she was also losing her ability to speak, she still responded with interest to what was happening around her. One day as a staff person was pushing her down the hall in her wheelchair, Sheila surprised and delighted us all by shouting out joyfully, "Oh, isn't life wonderful!"

As I hope these stories have shown, people with Alzheimer's disease can still give and receive love and can feel happiness and even joy, especially if these were part of the personality they had before they became ill. They sometimes also experience sadness, anger, grief, and frustration, as we all do from time to time. As the disease progresses, bodies and faces become more immobile until expressions of feeling may become so infrequent and subtle that they are missed by all but the most perceptive.

Educating ourselves about Alzheimer's in the event that we or someone we love might one day have the disease is part of being a friend to ourselves and to our loved ones. This falls into the same category as making out our will, choosing an executor, and completing a "living will" or directive to physicians. We make these preparations to ensure that our wishes are carried out and to relieve our families of the burden of guessing what they should do and what we want them to do. If Alzheimer's ever makes its drastic changes to your brain, you will not be able to make these decisions. Hard as it is, if you have had the courage to discuss your wishes about your death with your family members, then you can discuss the issue of dementia as well. And before you say "Just shoot me," take the time to see what programs are available and learn about the promising horizons of current research. With more knowledge about the illness come better treatments, training, support, and care facilities. Find out about these, and consider the possibility that having Alzheimer's is not always worse than suffering a paralyzing stroke or living with the excruciating pain of bones shattered by osteoporosis. If you can, spend one-on-one time with someone you have not previously known who has Alzheimer's disease. Even with mental impairments, we can still enjoy the gifts of love and laughter in the right environment with appropriate support and care.

If you suspect the onset of Alzheimer's, the first essential component of appropriate care is a medical and social services team that specializes in the diagnosis and follow-up care of people with dementia. The team may be an entire department at one of your local hospitals. Members of the team will be able to direct you and your family members to other support sources, such as the Alzheimer's Association, respite care, specialized facilities when and if they are needed, caregiver support groups, and educational information.

The second crucial component, if you have AD, is that you must be in a setting that is appropriate to your stage of the disease and your unique needs. This may be as simple as making sure you can't fall down the stairs in your home, or wander out onto the street unsupervised, or be able to turn on the stove. It may also include being in a care facility that is suited to your needs.

The third component is to have care providers who relate to you in an effective, patient, warm way. They must be trained in how to divert anger, how to move at a slower pace, and how to see you as you are with the disease rather than expect you to perform as you used to. Attentive sensitivity is crucial. Physical care matters, but if it is merely efficient and not accompanied by kindness and patience, you will feel as upset and diminished as any nonimpaired person would at not being heard and cared about.

The fourth determinant of the AD experience is what we bring to it ourselves by way of personal history. If you have been open to new experiences prior to the disease—that is, open in a way that thoughtfully explores and often accepts new ways of looking at yourself and the world—then you are probably going to fare better than people who have been rigid in their approach to life. If you have unresolved psychological issues, they will probably be freely expressed because your mind's censor will no longer exist.

Alzheimer's disease is not a one-size-fits-all proposition. Its specifics manifest differently with the individual. Neither does it fit into neat stages for everyone. Some people get it when they are already impaired with other disabilities; for others, it may be the first and only serious disability they have before they die. The average life expectancy from onset is four to eight years, but some people live with the disease for twenty years. There isn't one best setting or one best care plan that works for all who have it. Making sure our families know this, making sure they are prepared to advocate for what's best for our state of health and stage of the illness, is critical to our emotional experience and quality of life. This is why it's essential that we discuss the possibility with those who may one day be our guardians.

The Alzheimer's-stricken show us life without inhibition and without control. That this is so frightening to us is not surprising. From the beginning of our lives we are on a path of internally and externally mandated control. We learn to hold our heads upright, stand on wobbly legs, control our bowels, not touch anything breakable, not roam where we're not allowed. Conforming to the rules of behavior as laid down by our families, our schools, jobs, and society, we are gradually shaped into acceptably functioning adults. The lessons of control that have been part of our daily lives can fade gradually or in jerking flashes when our brains become damaged by disease, stroke, accident, or genetic predisposition. To those of us standing on the outside observing—we who are so profoundly inculcated with the rules, large and small, that give order and acceptance to our lives—this loss of inhibition and control is perceived as nothing less than the disintegration of all that shapes our time, our thoughts, our personality, and the behaviors that make us respectable adults. We view any functioning outside this structure as the worst of sins when chosen, the worst of tragedies when involuntary.

In the first chapter, "Befriending Yourself," I discussed how thoroughly we identify ourselves with our minds. Living in the information age makes us especially vulnerable to valuing the intellect above all else, which results in many of us never experiencing much of our whole selves. We may take our problems into psychotherapy only to hear the therapist say over and over, "That's what you *think,* what do you *feel?*" And we are often stymied by the question, because all we know is thinking. Our reliance on our minds to tell us who we are blinds us to the value and importance of the other powers and attributes of the self. The mind is a powerful and creative tool, and how we choose to use it impacts our experience and development—but still, it is not the whole self. It can enhance our lives immeasurably, but it can also ruin our lives and others' when used negatively, irresponsibly, or nefariously. By assuming that the mind is the only attribute that makes life worth living, we put all of our eggs in one basket, and when it falls, we lose everything we had counted on and are unable to perceive that anything of value might be left.

Losing our mind is more frightening to most of us than death. It's more than the fear of losing the tool that has propelled us into our current roles, status, and accomplishments, more than the humiliation of losing these important ways we are identified by society. We think of it as an annihilation worse than death because we assume that with dementia somehow we will continue to exist but *no longer as ourselves.* Unlike other disabilities, a mental impairment causes others to perceive the impaired person as *being* that impairment. We are more likely to label people as being their mental disease than to label people as being their physical disease, even though both are biologically based. To the unpracticed eye, the person with AD has become a "what" rather than a "who." It is our bias toward the mind and our deep identification with it that blinds us to the possibility that we could continue to find life worth living, even with Alzheimer's Disease.

Those of us who have worked with and befriended those stricken with mental impairments know that love and friendship, wonder, curiosity, and even joy are not the exclusive domain of the mentally gifted. If anything, the opposite often seems to be true. In a state of mental impairment we are often able to tap more deeply into our hearts than was ever possible when the mind was in control.

# Part II

## Spiritual Preparation

To tackle a general discussion of spirituality, as I do here in Part II, is to enter a potential minefield. The material in this section may seem offensive to those wedded to doctrine, whether it is traditional religion or new age. My intention is not to offend but to present some concepts large enough to facilitate our thinking about ourselves, the world, and our place in it. These ideas are intended to provoke your own pondering and exploration.

I have chosen to separate these ideas about spirituality from any particular religious or new age system because the institutionalization of spirituality alters it. Regardless of how good the organizers' intentions may be, most systems eventually assume an authority that shifts the focus from the spiritual growth of the individuals involved to the survival of the institution itself. In settings that tend toward legalistic rules and rigid beliefs, an individual's spiritual growth—which tends to be unpredictable and not fitting prescribed formulas—can be perceived as a threat to the stability of the group.

The pitfalls inherent in religious and new age institutions

are many. This fact is attested to by the many "walking wounded" whose disappointment, hurt, and anger at these establishments have driven them away. Unfortunately, it can also drive them away from any exploration of spirituality that would support their own growth. Some of these pitfalls are so subtle that many, including religious and spiritual leaders, do not see them. Thus many people do not find out that they are and have been living in a spiritually dry pit until they are old and sick, in serious need of spiritual resources, only to find out that none are forthcoming.

The emotional exploration and healing work we do is a path to the sacred. For myself, I found that the efforts I'd made at emotional clarity carried me to the threshold of the holy. From there, I experienced a shift of some kind as I crossed into an awareness of a new "space," where I discovered a depth of meaning and understanding that I can describe only as "spiritual." I had to come to that space with enough self-knowledge that I could partake of its richness without becoming too idealistic or otherwise distorting the reality of sacredness that I now sensed all around me.

We all know that horrible things have been done—and still are being done—in the name of someone's religion or god. Such acts are initiated by people who have not taken a healthy look at themselves and therefore have never become responsible for the motives behind their actions. I'll never forget my wonder when a self-described "good Christian" came to my church office asking for "ammunition." She wanted it to use on an older woman with dementia living in a nursing home who, although receiving treatment by good doctors, was still suffering from depression and the grief of widowhood. The "ammunition" that the woman was referring to was scripture; she planned to—I suppose—"shoot" the hurting widow with it and cure her of the melancholy that her circumstances gave her every right to have. It was apparent to me that this "good Christian" was totally unaware that the widow's feelings touched too close to her own loss and despair at having recently been widowed herself. Determined to hold on to the facade of a happy, fulfilled religious person, she needed ammunition to "kill" the feelings of the other woman before they unearthed her own pain and dissatisfaction. Although she was by nature a kind and caring person, to avoid experiencing her own vulnerability she had set herself up as a model of religious maturity and a counselor to others who appeared less strong. The trouble was that since she wouldn't allow herself to feel her own truth, her ministrations were not from the heart. They grew from the need to make herself feel and appear to be the better Christian. Many recipients of her attentions dreaded to see her coming.

When I speak of spirituality, I refer to an individual's sense of connection to something larger than the self. It may be larger than one's immediate community or national boundaries; for some it extends even beyond our species. While the exploration of our spirituality can make us acutely and often painfully aware of the dark side of ourselves and the world we live in, the exploration itself is a healthy process producing a state of heart and mind that reaches for understanding of life and self, forgiveness and healing.

Spirituality is as broad and varied as the number of people who encounter it—which is as it should be. While we may share common threads to our experience, we will, by our very nature, view any one of the innumerable facets of this phenomenon from our own unique experience and perspective. A familiarity with our personal spirituality will provide a framework that will help us find and maintain a sense of meaning and purpose, both today and when the changes of late life might otherwise overwhelm us. By paying attention to and learning about this dimension of ourselves in midlife, we can begin opening doors to a new level of being.

Spirituality doesn't require a belief in a god, although many choose to define it that way. Spirituality doesn't require a belief in life after death. I have known and worked with atheists who have lived meaningful, rich lives through deeply held spiritual values (although they did not necessarily describe them that way) and who believed their last breath was the end of them. And I have seen them die in great peace.

Some group connections make us feel valued, and sometimes superior, by supplying an otherwise nonexistent individual identity. Religious and new age organizations, gangs in poor neighborhoods, and social clubs in the upper echelons of society often function in this way. But the connectedness that I'm speaking of is not competitive, it does not foster feelings of superiority, it does not breed an "us against them" mentality. Rather, it supports a growing sense of oneness, a knowledge that all, including ourselves, are valuable and an important part of the bigger picture. This spirituality, or sense of connection, occurs in the most intimate part of us, a part so inexpressible that we often use metaphor when we can speak of it, and symbols or ritual when we cannot.

The descriptive words I use in the chapters to come are inadequate, as are all words used to refer to the numinous, which is defined in my *Random House Dictionary* as "spiritual or supernatural; surpassing comprehension or understanding; mysterious." I will use words such as "the holy," "sacred," "spirit," and "spirituality." These are words I am comfortable with, although they manage, always, to stay just beyond the reach of straightforward definitions. I also use the word "mystery" because for many people the concept of "God" has been made literal and trivial. God is often taught and experienced as a being made up of the best and worst projections of ourselves, a deity who requires worship, doctrines, and rules that may or may not be in the best interest of our souls. This god is little more than an idol to be appeased and won over. If this has been our religious experience, then we learn too late, when the chips are down and real desperation takes over, that an idol has nothing to give us.

A few of the chapters in Part II are considerably shorter than those in Part I. This is because the mind is the seat of language, and spirituality, as I experience it, is a function of the heart. The layers of meaning the heart can perceive are difficult and often impossible to filter through the mind to produce language adequate to the perception. I have deliberately refrained from wrapping the package too neatly, since each of us must find our own details on this journey of the heart. In that spirit, I have chosen to use lowercase letters for the names of deities and for spiritual and religious concepts, except when an individual uses such a term as a proper noun that has personal meaning. I also made an exception for "God" in the paragraph before this one, hoping not to startle my readers with my unusual system. My intent is to keep any one idea from seeming grander than the others: I believe each of them contains the seed of universal truth. My apologies to any who are offended by this choice.

For the purposes of this book, "religion" refers to the traditional religious as well as new age institutions and to their doctrines, beliefs, and rituals. Spirituality exists both inside and outside of these systems. An institution can nurture and support one's spirituality, but it can also stifle one's direct "knowing" of that which is holy. Legalistic, rigid systems of belief, peer pressure, and hypocrisy can lock us in at the most superficial levels of our spirit. Spirituality is bigger than any institution and assumes that each individual has direct access to the experience and expression of that which is sacred.

Like many people, I have art objects around my house and office to help me remember that there is more to life than meeting deadlines and paying bills. The sculpted snake that sits on the top of my computer monitor reminds me of the possibility of healing and transformation. The close-up photos on my desk of a mountain flower and a bumblebee are there to remind me that there is beauty and order to life as well as the sorrow and chaos I witness in the lives of my clients. I have artifacts from Judaic, Christian, Native American, Islamic, Hindu, and Buddhist religions, to remind me that the mystery is so big that it is perceived by all cultures in their own forms of expression. For me, participating in any ritual of sacred communion always brings me to my knees—figuratively and literally—in the remembrance of and recommitment to what I perceive to be sacred and my connection to it. It doesn't matter to me where or when it takes place, or even the context of the institutional belief. It is a ritual that is personal, moves me deeply, and serves as a reminder to my heart of how I want to be in the world.

But there is real danger in our symbols and rituals, a danger that we will forget that they are simply forms created to represent the substance of something larger. No matter what the experiences or beliefs—no matter whether they're formalized by churches, synagogues, mosques, monasteries, retreats, or our own private symbol and ritual—we must not forget that the forms are meant to represent something bigger than we can fully grasp. Too many of us, not even recognizing that we're doing it, end up worshiping the form, blind to the fact that its purpose is to point the way to something larger.

In the mid-1970s I met a woman who was a disciple of Sai Baba, a holy man in India. She had lived at his religious retreat and residence for years, attending his daily audiences and faithfully following all he taught. Or so she thought. One day as he walked among the hundreds of disciples who came daily to hear his teachings, he stopped in front of this woman and told her that instead of moving in the direction his teachings pointed, she had settled for worshiping him. He said it was the same as climbing a signpost on the mistaken assumption that it was the destination rather than an invitation to move in the direction it pointed.

Like mistaking the finger pointing at the moon for the moon itself, there are many of us clinging to religious and new age signposts, imbuing them with power and promise they were never intended to have. When we do this our journey ends at the sign, instead of allowing it to direct us into the new territory to which it is trying to lead us. For far too many people, religion is a spectator sport from the foot of a signpost. Having settled there, we attend services and take part in rituals regularly, never realizing that the teachings are meant to push us into deeper territories of self and spirit and to impact the choices we make about how we will live our daily lives.

For those who haven't understood the nature and purpose of belief, symbol, and ritual—and unfortunately this includes many who teach them—a crisis can bring desperation when they find that all they counted on to pull them through is simply not there. It's especially heartbreaking to see this happen at the end of life, when investment in the forms has been longstanding and the heart and mind have been stifled for decades by the belief or instruction to park at the signpost. Some religious and new age systems may even imply that doing anything else—like moving in the direction to which the symbol and ritual are leading—is heresy.

Audrey is a tragic example of someone who never looked beyond the forms of her religion. The nursing home staff asked me to see Audrey, a small, attractive woman in her late seventies, a few days after her middle-aged son died of cancer. Death was no stranger to Audrey. Years earlier her daughter had been killed in a mountaineering accident shortly after Audrey had awakened one morning to find her husband dead in bed beside her, having had no warning of his impending heart attack. Now, after her son's death, she wasn't eating and sleep was eluding her.

Audrey's life had centered around her church. Everything that had happened, she told me, was "God's will." According to her personal belief system, if she truly loved and served God, she was not allowed to question that will or even to feel bad about it. During several sessions with her I pointed out that even Jesus grieved, expressed anger, and experienced the absence of God. But she insisted that since all of it was God's will, she was not bothered by any of her losses. As she told me that she felt just fine, tears were leaking from her eyes and trickling silently past her sweet smile. The energy it took for her to be faithful to her rigid understanding killed her appetite and tore at her nerves. She died in less than a year, having repressed her devastation and grief. In essence, her belief system, as she understood it, killed her.

Two other women, more familiar with the truth of their feelings, confided from their nursing home beds that they felt abandoned and betrayed by their God. Both had been faithful to their religious communities all of their lives. Now, one was chronically ill and disabled, and the other, recently widowed, was terminally ill. Both of them were experiencing severe physical discomfort and couldn't understand why God would not let them die. I asked each woman if she had talked about this with her minister or priest, both of whom called on their parishioner regularly. Each woman said she hadn't. They had told their clergy what they thought they were supposed to say. They were afraid if they confided their true feelings, their minister and priest would judge them as having a lack of faith and thus being unworthy of God's help. I knew both of their clergy and knew that they were compassionate men, so it saddened me that these women felt they couldn't share their feelings with their religious guides. Their denial was, I think, a last act of loyalty to a fearsome idol/god that they couldn't trust without fear of reprisal.

When I made the decision to go to seminary and become an ordained minister, the name "God" was for me a shorthand term for something bigger and more complex than I could fathom. To my surprise and dismay, at some point in the course of my six years as church pastor, "God" became anthropomorphized in my mind as I used the language of the institution. I discovered at a crisis point that my personal god had turned into an old man in the sky who, although described as loving, often seemed arbitrary and cranky. I had to lose this idea of "God" and find mystery again.

Spirituality is a moving target and, like religion, should never be merely a spectator sport, not if we want the deeper dimensions of life where meaning and purpose reside. Spirituality is like a deer that slowly leads us deeper into the forest—we must move with care and attention, stopping often to listen for the clues as to where we are, how we are, and in which direction we are being led.

It is my hope that the principles offered in this section will be the trailheads or signposts for your own exploration. They may be applied both within and outside of any existing religious tradition. The goal is to evolve a working faith, a set of values, and an understanding or philosophy big enough to encompass the realities of our entire lives. Whether you are an atheist or an agnostic, whether you are a member of a religious tradition or an adherent to some other way in which the sacred expresses itself, I hope the ideas in this section will be an inspiration for the growth and exploration of your own unique and beautiful spirit.

# 5

# Evolving Toward
# True North

"True north" is a term used in navigation to signify the north-ernmost point on the planet. With a compass and charts, navigators are able to locate true north, the major reference point for determining where they are and what direction their course must take.

In this chapter I use "true north" as a metaphor for the state of completion we can attain before we die. True north, or completion, is the topmost point of our lives, our destination, and a reference point we can use for guiding our current decisions. I will talk about evolving values that will function as a compass to help us find our current spiritual location and determine the course toward our destination. Having completion as our chosen destination will itself help us discover and evolve the values that will realign us when we are in danger of wavering from our desired course.

Our true north is who we want to become before we die—our personal state of completion. Having this vision will help us shift our primary focus from an external to an internal landscape.

Like the many navigators who find their way around the planet without having actually visited true north, we will journey until our last stage of life, carrying the vision of our eventual completion to inspire us and keep us on course. Your true north is, as one elder put it, "where you can hang your heart when your brain has done its logical best and failed." And like the men and women who rely on directional instruments as they travel the physical world, we too will need tools, and the skills to use them, to help us stay on course or find it again when we lose it. Over time and with practice, the instruments that will help you stay aligned to your true north will become the internal guides with which you can direct your course of action for the rest of your life.

Early in my training as a hospital chaplain a group of us were told to write down the ten most important things that made our lives worth living. After much thought, I wrote down each of my children, the sky, the trees, my health, and I don't remember what else—this took place more than twenty years ago. After we'd finished our lists, the leader told us that circumstances dictated that we had to give up one item and cross it off our list. There was a stunned silence, then consternation as our heads bent to our lists and we tried to decide which item would be easiest to live without. After much time we raised our now sober faces to learn why we'd had to do this. With no explanation the facilitator said that new circumstances required that we had to eliminate two more items. The serious silence that followed this statement was broken by a groan from somewhere in the room. It took longer to make these two difficult decisions, but having finally done so, we waited for an explanation. "Two more things have to go," he informed us, and now groans of indignation and grief were emitted from all sides of the room. The exercise continued until we were left with only two of the items that made our lives worth living. My list now consisted of the names of my two sons. "You have to give up one of the two things you have left," the facilitator intoned. I froze, frantic and outraged. How could I choose between my children? What kind of cruelty was this? In silent, mutinous anger, I crossed my arms over my chest, refusing to even touch the pencil that would eliminate one of my children. The last instruction was to cross off the one remaining item on our list.

The point of the exercise was, of course, to sensitize us to what a dying person is losing. Even though it was a simulated situation, it evoked strong emotions in all of us. As each item was crossed off we could see our lives becoming more restricted, less meaningful, more difficult to imagine, and finally without meaning at all.

What I didn't know at the time, and only learned in my years of relating to elders, is that it's possible for an individual to have an internal foundation that transcends loss—*please note that I did not say it eliminated grief.* This foundation consists of the vision of our completed self and the tools to move in that direction. It is our guide and the carrier of our unique purpose and meaning, even in the worst of times. With these tools and the skills for their use, we will be able to keep our vessel on course in the roughest seas and bring it back to equilibrium when it threatens to tip over. What having that foundation *doesn't* do is prevent the pain and grief that life will bring us anyway.

Some day, in the natural course of things, we will lose everything and everyone we care about. For most of us those losses will come slowly, over a period of years. But even if stretched out over a long period of time they are painful, often devastating, to experience. Beginning now, we have the opportunity to develop a vision of our true north and the values—our compass—that will ensure progress in our travels. With these in place we will be more likely to regain our bearings when change, loss, and unfamiliar circumstances threaten to overwhelm us, and we are more likely to arrive at our destination, finding peaceful harbors for rest, repair, and replenishment of depleted stocks along the way.

In middle age, many of us are finally meeting society's definition of success. This is also a time when many of us are beginning to take stock of where we are and where we're headed. We may begin to realize now that something is missing in our lives or anticipate that it will be missing in the not-distant-enough future. We may become aware of an emptiness, a hollow feeling, somewhere in our gut or heart. This vacuum may cause us to wonder if, when all's been said and done, the priorities and goals we have been living by are adequate—if they are worthy of our "one wild and precious life."[11] For most of us, obligations, goals imposed by duty, and many other distractions have kept us occupied. But now, at midlife, we may begin to sense a shift in our inner tides and find, at our core, a vast and lifeless mudflat.

To ignore that barren place inside that is trying to tell us something is missing is to anchor ourselves in the spiritual murkiness of unasked and unanswered questions. The unasked and unanswered will, over the years, slowly drag us down into depression, frustration, and angst. We can continue to stay so busy and distracted that we are always one step ahead of our feelings and blind to our long-term future. Or we can make ourselves numb with one of the many addictions that plague our society, among them workaholism, consumerism, television, food, gambling, drugs, and alcohol. But our dread, anxiety, and anguish will grow silently, bleeding away contentment from our lives. The vitality and curiosity that make us truly alive will die: we will become one of the living dead. And when we finally arrive at our last years, we will have no purpose, meaning, or completion, and nothing inside to sustain us.

Whatever our choices have been, many of us have managed to survive and even thrive into middle age. We have made a place for ourselves in the world. Now many are wondering, "Is this all there is?" or "Who will I be when I am no longer able to do the things I do now?" Painful as these questions are, they are the mark of maturity, of a heart and mind no longer willing to settle for face value. This is the beginning of wisdom.

We may experience this point as nothing more than floundering, moving about with no direction, wondering if there's something else we should be doing next. But this very uncertainty allows us to pay attention to the questions that appear in the emptiness, if we listen for them. Watching these questions evolve and discovering where they lead us will eventually shape our floundering and the "mudflat" into a meaningful form.

"Floundering," by the way—feeling lost in the midst of the familiar—is a positive state to be in. This is when we are more likely to ask the hard questions about the ultimate point of what we are doing with our lives. It is when we are most likely to be open to considering living our lives based on lasting values and discovering what those values might be. It's a time of waking up to explore and experiment until we find the true north that will set the tone and direction of the rest of our lives.

Twenty-five years ago my true north was the desire to minister to life. This value was so strong and compelling that

I went to college so I could attend seminary after gradua-
tion—this in spite of the fact that I was a single mother of two
children with barely enough money to feed us. I pushed
beyond my perceived limitations of skill, energy, and ade-
quacy. My hope and vision were profoundly affirmed by my
seminary degree and ordination as minister and pastor of a
church. Having moved to another state to take up these duties,
however, I was terribly lonely, as I mentioned in the chapter on
grief, as well as terrified that my abilities were not sufficient to
live up to my own, and others', expectations.

When I arrived, the congregation was very small, but in
the first few years of my ministry we became the fastest-
growing church in the denomination's two-state region. The
tithes and offerings grew so large that we were able to pay
cash for a new education wing. All of this growth came by
word of mouth; we didn't have membership drives, we
weren't even listed in the phone book. Soon the old members
were outnumbered three to one by new people.

But the church, which had been founded ninety years earlier, had unwritten rules. The primary rule was that the power
in the church was held not by the pastor and the church coun-
cil but by a few families who had been in the church for
decades. The new people, as unaware of this situation as I was,
assumed that as the minister I was also the leader. It took
them, like me, some time to realize that nothing important
could happen without the consent and cooperation of this old
guard.

Finally, feeling threatened by the growth that was under-
mining their power, the old guard went into action. When the
attack came, it was personal and directed at me—they took
things I said out of context and gave them a different inter-
pretation. They accused me of statements I had never made

and of behaviors in which I would never think of engaging. For the next year and a half they constantly questioned and criticized my actions and intentions. Although few in number, these people wielded their power and made my life hell. Maybe I *should have* weathered the storm—but I was so demoralized by the assault that when I was approached with an offer for employment as a full-time counselor at the retirement center, I quickly accepted.

The events at the church were more devastating to me than I could ever have put into words. During my years of struggling with single parenthood, getting through college and seminary, and my years at the church, I had given the best of everything I had to a larger purpose I deeply believed in. In the end, I left the church battered to the core, my belief system and faith shattered. I stumbled through the first months of the new job exhausted and numb. I took long walks at night to feel my body and smell the fresh air to prove I was still alive. I felt the pain that darkened and chilled every corner of my heart. Relief from despair came only while I counseled clients. In those times I was able to move out of my own despair to attend to theirs.

Several months into my new job, I noticed, on a late-night walk, that something had changed. I felt a tiny warm place, like a very small flame, within me. "What is this?" I wondered. Several night walks later I was able to identify it—it was a small flame of kindness, caring, and love that had grown during my counseling of other wounded human beings. I had moved from being only a minister and counselor to listening from my own wounded depths to the realities with which we all struggle. I understood then, as never before, that life events often batter and shatter us, no matter how deep our integrity, how sincere our commitment and intention. The tiny flame was sending its small light into the darkness of my heart, gently illuminating and warming the empty place that had once housed my faith and dedication. I was astounded and relieved to discover that the little flame—a small love—was sufficient to give meaning and purpose to my life. This was an evolution and a realignment of the compass that guides me toward my true north.

I continued with my expanding professional duties, using this value to determine my decisions in life and relationships. Love has become the internal compass that I seek when I feel lost or confused about which direction to move in, which choices to make, and what behavior on my part is appropriate to the situation. As I return again and again to this value, it continues to evolve and becomes easier to use as a guide. This is not to say that I am always on course or that I have become a meek and mild person, nor does it mean that I was without love before. This value is a natural outgrowth of the earlier aspiration to minister to life, with another evolution in between, which I will speak of a little later.

A vision of personal completion and the values that guide us to it will always seek truth no matter what the circumstances. But to remain authentic we must sometimes ask hard questions of these assumptions in order to test the relevancy of our vision and values. Completion requires different values from society's, so they will remain relevant and appropriate even when we are taken out of the mainstream by poor health, financial straits, disability, or eventual old age. While we are still mobile and healthy, the vision of our completion will inspire us to make decisions that may appear foolish to others. For instance, you may decide to quit your high-powered job for a less demanding one. Your reasons may include wanting the energy to do volunteer work and having time to spend with your family. You may decide that driving a secondhand Dodge is preferable to making the payments on a BMW. Going against the prevailing definitions of "success"—money, title, material goods—requires courage and effort. You may find you won't receive much support for these decisions.

My true north obliges me to be aware of consequences to myself and to others of whatever decisions or actions I take. It's what I turn to especially when I feel I have been treated unjustly or that someone is trying to manipulate me. I no longer accept these behaviors. By remembering my vision and the value that is my major reference point, I can, with determination and sometimes great difficulty, draw the line and hold my ground with self-respect that does not denigrate the person who has offended me. My true north—when I refer to it for direction—also makes it clear when my hurt and angry feelings are hardening into pride and self-righteousness. When I sense this happening, I have to decide how long I can allow myself the luxury of a grudge without hurting myself emotionally and spiritually. This helps me to let go of my hurt and to appreciate other people's struggles, including the fact that manipulation or bullying may be the only way they ever learned how to get what they need.

Discovering and allowing the evolution of values that will carry you toward your own completion can take quite a while. The small warm place in my heart that was love was built on earlier values I had named and used as my guides for a long time. Surviving, earning approval, finding love, and being kind were the goals of my early decades. Those slowly transformed into ministering to life. Ministering to life evolved further into being a healing presence. Currently, all of these have coalesced into, simply, love. I fully expect my understanding to grow and evolve as I explore and live by this value.

A woman I know lives by one commandment—her value and compass—which is, "Thou shalt not violate." The implications of this value are universal. It informs her actions toward other people, toward the environment and all the creatures who live there. It also carries the imperative of taking care of herself so that she does not violate her own being. Life being what it is, she is often in the position of having to choose the lesser violation. Sometimes, no matter what action she takes, it will have a negative impact somewhere. If she comes home very late at the end of an exhausting day, for example, she might decide the best choice is to care for herself. She'll take a hot bath and climb into bed rather than sorting and carrying her recyclables down to the curb. She'll recycle for next month's pickup, or maybe she'll wait until her current work project is finished and she is not so tired. Her commitment to her "Thou shalt not violate" commandment causes her to pay close attention to her choices and their consequences. Using the commandment as her guide, she can more easily make decisions that maintain her wholeness as well as the integrity of life around her.

Many people have service to others as their core value, and we would be a heartless world without it. As I mentioned in the chapter "You Always Make a Difference," the life on this planet is held together by a web of people making grassroots efforts to be of service. If this is your compass value, you must be prepared to define and redefine what "service" is in each situation. A nursing home housekeeper shows her sensitive attunement to service when she asks patients who are having a bad day if they'd rather not converse and if they'd prefer she come back later to clean. "Sometimes," she says, "the best way to care for and respect someone is to leave the person alone for a while." If service is our reference point, we will need this kind of sensitivity and the ability to discern what action or inaction truly serves those we want to assist. When we are in our last stage of life, if we find ourselves without the physical or financial resources to perform service in the ways that were once familiar to us, then we will have to redefine what service we can provide in that circumstance. The opportunity to serve will always be available to us, even when we are old and disabled.

Let me refer you back again to the chapter "You Always Make a Difference," in which I described the experience of one nursing home resident in an emotional slump. Adrift and bitter about being dependent, she finally decided she had to take a different tack or she would only make herself and those around her more miserable. She resolved to do everything she could to make the people who cared for her feel appreciated. With practice, her own appreciation solidified and the new value took hold in her heart. Her life once again had meaning and purpose and supported her in becoming the person she wanted to be.

However your values, which will be your compass, may evolve, it will take a lot of trial and error to discover them and years of testing in the various life situations in which you find yourself. The first step is to pay very close attention to the truth behind your actions and feelings. Even if they look saintly on the surface, the motivation that drives even the apparently good behaviors may not be so benign. This might include manipulation to attain a goal of power and obligation over others. Our "selfless" actions may be done so we'll look good or be important or maybe so we'll be loved and admired. Manipulation may be second nature to us, or it may be the result of being raised in a culture that values appearances over honesty and integrity. In any case, paying deep attention to what really lives behind your choices is the only way to find out where you are. You have to know where you are before you can make thoughtful and conscious decisions about where you want to go and who and what you want to be. This attention to self has to be done with kindness so that—as I mentioned in an earlier chapter—you will feel safe enough to acknowledge your own truth.

As you explore your direction, ask yourself: "Does this help me show up for my life with integrity? Does it support my physical, mental, emotional, and spiritual health? Does it create congruency and harmony in myself and toward others? Is it moving me in the direction of my own completion?" If you find that what you aspire to causes you to be dishonest in any way—including dishonest with yourself—then it's not going to help you attain anything of lasting value. If you profess a belief, philosophy, or theology that doesn't quite square with what seems real and right to you, then it cannot be the well-functioning and practical guide you will need to help you through tough times. Neither will you find internal strength by conforming, consciously or unconsciously, to corporate, friends', or family expectations that leave you feeling compromised, exhausted, or—worse—"crazy."

We can fool ourselves with a set of values that were never our own and not even know it, as long as we don't look too carefully at how we feel and at what's in that space at our center. A friend of mine has been bored with his profession for the thirty years I've known him. For all that time he's been saying he wants out. He did, in fact, leave the job at one point and begin exploring possible new careers. But soon he got scared—being unemployed went against the work ethic he'd been raised with. When another corporation aggressively tried to hire him to fill a position identical to the one he had left, he broke down and took the job, despite the fact that he had accumulated ample savings to see him through a career transition. Now, years later, he is even more bored and miserable than he was at the old job. His salary is so high that he says he can't afford to quit, even with his considerable assets. But I see a person who has had serious health problems in the last couple of years and is not happy with his life because he hates his work. His once wonderful sense of humor has dulled and retreated, appearing far less often than it used to. His playful and happy personality has given way to short-temperedness and a sense of powerlessness over his own destiny. He is paying for his high salary and his unhealthy work ethic with his life—past, present, and future. From the standpoint of one who loves him, it is far too great a price to pay.[12]

Many of us get ourselves into situations—jobs, relationships, activities—based on values that may or may not be our own. Because we've been led to believe these are the "right" values, we act in accordance with them, assuming that following them will not only make us "right" but make us happy as well.

You will ultimately be damaged by the adoption of any assumptions, expectations, rules, or beliefs that violate what your heart and mind know or suspect to be true. Living with the consequences of dishonesty always necessitates more of it to support the original lie. Having to squander your personal energy resources in this way denies you the freedom of authenticity—the unencumbered mind and heart that is necessary if you are to participate freely in life. When you are old and no longer participating in society's mainstream, you may have years in which to regret the missed opportunities for authentic living.

I have been in some disastrous situations in my life

because, for a long time, I was using a template of values I inherited. I assumed these were the only "right" standards whether they made sense to me or not, and I thought that living in accordance with them made me prudent and worthy. Some of these values were so superficial that they directed me—and other young women of my generation—to choose a life partner based on his looks, height, and age. The men we dated were supposed to be good-looking, taller than we were, and preferably a few years older. Hardy couples who recognized quality over appearance and bucked these superficial expectations by dating and even marrying each other usually took a ribbing, at least behind their backs. Thank goodness that has changed!

It took me a long time to figure out that many of the values I had unconsciously assumed did not always serve me well in improving the quality of my experiences. This awareness was years in coming, but finally I learned to pay attention to my internal life and take it seriously, both its satisfactions and its conflicts. The process took a quantum leap forward when I was first able to articulate an internal goal that would guide me toward growing into a healing presence—the value that later evolved to "love." The clarity this internal standard has already afforded me, even as it continues to evolve, has allowed me to use my emotional energy more efficiently than ever before. Sometimes when I am tired, hurt, scared, or angry, living up to my guiding principle of love takes great effort. But having it as a reference point saves me from a lot of confusion and wasted energy.

It took the disaster at the church for me to discover that my theology had tilted to a literal sense of the holy. Painful as the realization was, it allowed me to move to a deeper level and to the evolution of an internal value that keeps me on course toward completion. Being a healing presence was, and still is, a powerful compass for me. But its evolution to what I experience as the less grandiose "love" made a profound difference in how I have organized my thinking about my spiritual location and direction. For one thing, as this value has continued to evolve, I am finally learning that "love" includes loving myself. If I don't take care of my own physical, emotional, and spiritual needs for rest, recreation, nutrition, exercise, and solitude as well as time with friends, then whatever love I hope to offer is filtered through exhaustion and sometimes even resentment. When I am fatigued, I may still feel love, but it is smaller and weaker and in danger of becoming a mere mechanical action.

When I was caught in the maelstrom at the church, I was focused on being a healing presence and didn't recognize the necessity of standing up to those who were damaging both me and the congregation. I was exhausted, discouraged, and nearly drowning in confusion about what course to take, because, in that situation, being a healing presence was not enough. It didn't protect me, nor did it protect the congregation from the forces that eventually tore it apart. Yes, love is hearts and valentines, support and affirmation. But love is also a mother bear protecting her young and herself. I had not yet identified this important aspect of love, had not yet included it in my understanding of my compass. Whether it would have changed the outcome or not, I cannot say, but it's possible that if I had been respectfully tough and confrontational, the damage to the congregation and to me would not have been so severe.

Discovering and exploring the values that keep you moving in the direction of your completion, and allowing their evolution, is a process of expansion and reduction, of starting with what you think works and then testing it in real-life situations to see if it really does. In its early stages the process may consist primarily of elimination; think of a sculptor carving away material to get to the shape that's inside.

Getting to our true north is an active process that includes paying attention to how events, people, ideas, and places affect us, both internally and externally, and then making choices based on what supports the best of who we are in the world. It's a shift from external rules to the development of internal principles of integrity. Like me, you may settle on a major reference point or value that works well for years and then find that life circumstances will bring about its refinement or transformation. This evolution will continue and will guide us into deeper levels of integrity right up until our last breath, if we are willing to pay attention and receive its teaching as the sacred process that it is. In this way we remain active participants in the unfolding of our life and consciousness, including our old age.

This always growing internal guide must be in place and we must be skilled at using it before we arrive at the last years of our lives, when our losses will be many. Trying to find and learn how to use a compass is impossible when the vessel is overwhelmed by threatening seas. No craft would venture to enter unpredictable waters without having this expertise already in place. Likewise, if we are to remain intact emotionally and spiritually when we are old and possibly dependent, we must face the facts of the rough seas we are going to enter and the toll they will exact if we are not prepared.

One elder's question still cuts my heart with the hopelessness it contained. Ardis had had a stroke that had left one side of her body permanently paralyzed. She had spent more than a year engaged in the extremely difficult and often discouraging work of relearning how to dress and groom herself, how to eat, and how to transfer from wheelchair to toilet to bed, but she had persevered and was now able to live independently in her own apartment in a facility that offered her the assistance she occasionally needed. One day she joined a discussion I was having with a group of the facility's residents. The conversation had turned to the subject of what events lent pleasure to life in spite of limitation and disability. Ardis remained quiet until she threw her question across the room like an unfurling black banner: "What's the point of life if all you do is spend the day maintaining yourself?" Conversation stopped dead as each of us sat with the echo of the question only she could answer for herself. What was there to say to this woman who could not see beyond what she had lost to what she had achieved? Always temperamental and difficult, she had developed a bitter, cruel streak since her stroke and sometimes reduced vulnerable residents to tears by her infliction of vicious, rejecting words. I marveled at the stubbornness and endurance it had taken for her to achieve her current level of independence. I knew that this work of rehabilitation, of relearning, is as hard as or harder than any other we are called on to do in our lives. For example, when a person is paralyzed on one side, dressing—which used to take maybe five minutes—now takes an hour or two hours to complete. It is more frustrating than a nonparalyzed person can imagine.

In Western society and in her own eyes, Ardis was just a paralyzed old woman. In my eyes, through her physical accomplishments, she was a hero. But her inability to see beyond the surface of her situation had so limited her emotional experience that she had no viable inner direction for herself. She was unable to recognize or feel pride in what she had achieved, and her bitterness kept her from recognizing the potential for friendship in the people around her. Instead she wreaked her verbal and sometimes physical vengeance on any who were unfortunate enough to get in her way. As of this writing she has lived in this state and with this attitude for nine years, with no sign that death is coming anytime soon. She is not a bad person, only an unprepared one lacking crucial emotional and spiritual skills. What a tragic way to experience the last years of one's life!

Life circumstances demand that we change as we age. Think of it as a process of staying emotionally and spiritually flexible so that we don't get permanently stuck in a dead end or wedded to a belief that may fit some circumstances but is too small to encompass all of our experience. The ongoing search for more depth of understanding that allows our values to expand and deepen is truly a spiritual practice. Any belief or set of beliefs that we have not explored, questioned, or tested against real-life situations will bring our potential for spiritual growth to a standstill. Our spiritual evolution while journeying toward completion is the verb of who we are and what we bring to the world.

Suffering can be a fast lane to understanding. Perhaps this is the mechanism that exists somewhere deep in the angst, anxiety, and depression felt by so many in our society. Suffering can be a dangerous road, however. Along with being a great motivator for change, pain makes us vulnerable to timidity, bitterness, vengefulness, clinical depression, addiction, and suicide.

For those whose difficult life circumstances have pushed them far beyond the boundaries of healthy human experience, the path to understanding is neither straight nor fast. You may have been on the road of suffering for so long that exhaustion has killed hope. Emotional and spiritual pain may have overwhelmed and paralyzed you, or driven you into behavior that is destructive to yourself and probably to others as well. If this is the case, not only your mental and spiritual health but your physical health and your very life may be at stake. "God doesn't give us more than we can handle" is a nice sentiment, but it is not a Biblical quote (though many assume it is), nor is it true. I have seen people emotionally overwhelmed and destroyed by what has happened to them. Research of the past ten years has uncovered the fact that psychological trauma and suffering can alter one's biology. When life circumstances create too much stress, our physiological response is to flood our body and brain with the hormones involved in the stress response. A physiology that is constantly awash with these chemicals can be seriously damaged.

Fortunately, there is help. With intervention and treatment these damaged parts of us can be supported and stabilized. The recent research into psychological trauma and stress has produced new medications and therapies that heal. In addition, there are the ancient healing arts of acupuncture, Chinese herbs, naturopathy, cranio-sacral work, and other therapies that can also be very effective. New understanding of how emotional suffering and severe stress affect people has also produced mental health professionals with specialized training and skill to facilitate the healing of these wounds. Combining appropriate medications and other treatments with psychotherapeutic support provides the best chance emotionally traumatized people have ever had to manage the unspeakable events they have experienced.

If you are one of these walking wounded, I applaud the courage it has taken for you to get this far in life, knowing what it has cost you most days simply to get out of bed. Give yourself a break—access the assistance you need and deserve. For medications I urge you to consult a psychiatrist who specializes in depression and psychological trauma issues. Prescribing medications is an art, and requires a great deal of skill and sensitivity to your situation. If long- or short-term emotional trauma is part of your history, make sure your psychotherapist specializes in working with these issues because they are significantly different from those of normal neurosis. And remember that while some professionals are quite gifted, others should have taken up a different line of work. You must feel comfortable, safe, respected, and heard by a doctor or therapist. If you don't feel these, then don't waste any more money or time with this person. If you have been terrorized by psychological trauma, your issues *are* comfort, safety, respect, and being heard. Unsympathetic professionals who don't listen to you reinforce the feelings of powerlessness you have already experienced. No matter how many framed diplomas and certificates a doctor or therapist has on the wall, if he or she is not sympathetic, he or she does not have the capacity for healing. Remember, too, that having had your experience, you know more about life than those who have never suffered. This is both a blessing and a curse, depending on whether you honor what you know and have survived or beat yourself up because you're different.

I have always disliked the idea that we are being "tested" by a deity when something awful happens to us. Bad things happen, and none of us are exempt from the possibility that they will come to us as well. I have pondered a different possibility inherent in crisis that in no way changes the fact that it is a genuine disaster: perhaps the events that devastate us carry within them the seeds of spiritual "initiation" into a level of knowing we would not otherwise achieve.

Whether we are survivors of trauma or are experiencing general angst, if we honor the pain and reality of these and allow them to point us to our central core, we will discover what is true for us and thereby be opened to a new glimpse of life. After all, this pain is telling us—as all pain does—that something is out of balance or broken and needs attending to.

Finding our way to completion is not primarily a work of the intellect. It involves instinct, intuition, and quite possibly a full range of emotions from joy to despair. It requires facing up to the ghosts that have always caused us to run away from this inner part of ourselves. It's a work of the heart, which has its own logic—a logic that is often more viable and moral than the rationality of the mind. The mind is trained to help us "make it" in the world, and thereby tends to play by the world's rules. Our developing central core has the potential for discernment of meaning and value, a discernment that cannot be accomplished by the intellect alone. In order to grow at these deeper levels, we have to allow ourselves to be touched by life's joy as well as its grief.

# 6

# Finding a Larger Context
# for Your Life

If we don't have a sense of connection to anything outside of our immediate circle, we are living in a vacuum that contains only ourselves. When we are old, if we have lived this way, we will have only our disappointments, losses, aches, and pains to define our last years. Everything that is missing, everything we suffer—even minor inconveniences—will be magnified. We will not be able to conceptualize any possibility of meaning. As we try to adjust to living with the physical limitations of old age, despair will break our spirit if we don't have a broader view of life and our place in it.

In this chapter I want to talk about the importance of having a larger context for our lives, a context that incorporates all of life, extending beyond us but also containing us. Think of the larger context as a huge map whose territory includes the topography of your inner self as well as the universe, however large you perceive that to be. Relating to something larger than ourselves provides shape and structure to our lives, inspires us, and informs our values, goals, and behaviors. When we have a larger context within which to live, we will experience ourselves as being part of a multidimensional whole that is far bigger than the concerns of our daily lives.

Experience, intuition, and spiritual "knowing" are how we perceive our larger context. Trial and error, paying attention to how we really feel about our lives, and asking open-ended questions regarding the possible meanings of events—these are part of the process of finding it. We won't get hard-and-fast answers; there aren't any. The purpose of this exploration is to expand our vision. Using both our heart and our mind, we will learn to recognize which ideas and beliefs help us live with integrity. We are looking for what makes sense in our relationship to the whole. Worshiping our beliefs, our station in life, our possessions, or even a concept of god that is not congruent with our experience is not something we can afford to do if we are to keep growing. Our heart, if we consult it, will let us know if things are not right.

The theologian Walter Wink compares exploring a subject with the intellect alone to dissecting a frog. You pin it down, cut open its belly, slice its limbs, and study what you find there. In the end you may know a lot about the frog's various parts, but what you're left with is a dead frog. You've lost the "frogness" of the creature—the essence of its life and function.

The "frogness" of your own larger context may be totally inexplicable to anyone else, but you will know in your gut if it's right and true for you. If you want the "frogness" of your spirituality to stay vital, be prepared for an experience that will never stay fixed but will always be fluid. New aspects and possibilities will continue to become available as your awareness expands to "see" more. What we are talking about is ultimately a mystery. Whether your larger context is the human race, nature, the universe, or a higher power, you'll never understand it all. Accept what seems right for now, knowing that whatever your perceptions of a larger context are, they must remain open-ended if you are to continue your spiritual expansion, growing always, toward completion.

A larger context does not have to be symbolized by a deity; it may simply be our sense of connection to all of life, a vision of ourselves as part of life's natural cycles. Seeing ourselves as participants in these natural cycles will enable us to reconcile ourselves more easily to the changes that come with age. If we *don't* have this larger vision, in fact, when difficult things happen to us we may fall prey to the painful suspicion that we have been singled out to suffer by an unkind universe or deity.

When we are conscious of being part of a wider universe, we can begin to see that what we do matters. Every action we take has a consequence somewhere, whether good or bad. Everything that happens affects a part of the whole body of life. Having this knowledge of being part of something larger may motivate us to contribute to the greater good in whatever ways we can.

My most painful experience of being part of a larger picture came when my older son was in the Gulf War. I had the unexpected experience of feeling connected to all the mothers in history who saw their children off to war knowing that their "goodbye" might be the last one ever. I wept for Iraqi mothers as well as myself. I felt so much rage and grief that I could concentrate only when listening to news broadcasts. There was some small consolation in stitching together a quilt of mourning, spotting it with tears while glued to CNN every evening after work. Thankfully, the war was a short one and I didn't finish the quilt. But if the war had lasted longer and my son had been killed, the quilt of mourning would have been his coffin's cover. I was acutely conscious of the inconsolable bitterness and grief of mothers with only a flag to substitute for their dead children. I fantasized that if all the mothers involved showed up on the battlefield instead of their children, it would have been an even shorter conflict, because the unruly rage and grief we mothers felt would drive the tyrants of *all* the countries involved into hiding, if we didn't tear them limb from limb first. Then we could celebrate and go home and enjoy our families in peace.

There are many names for and experiences of a larger context. I don't think it matters what we call it; every culture has its own expression for it, and within each culture individuals have their own experience of it. Whatever we perceive as our larger context, it has to be real to us and sufficient for our unique lives.

Allen, a scientist in his mid-seventies and a self-proclaimed atheist, was diagnosed with a virulent cancer. The news came as an unwelcome shock to everyone because Allen was an active community leader and very much involved with his scientific affiliations. But Allen believed that everything he had learned in his life was now part of a collective human knowledge. He had approached his work intent on improving the general quality of life and was gratified by the knowledge that his discoveries could be built upon by others. This belief was his larger context. The satisfaction of knowing that he had made a difference, and was still doing so, gave him motivation beyond any thought of personal gain. Although he was deeply grieved about leaving his family, he was never despairing or depressed. Certain to the end that his ashes would be all that was left of him (and he requested that they be used to fertilize a tree), Allen remained curious and cheerful until his peaceful death.

And there was Donald, a brilliant clergyperson, former missionary, world traveler. He was the author of several books and working on another when cancer called a halt to everything that was normal about his life. In his remaining months he and I talked about what was happening to him, his regrets and his accomplishments. We talked about how his soon-to-be widow would fare; he worried about his grown children struggling in an unfriendly economy. We speculated about the possibility that he could still love and support them after he died. His face lit up at this thought. There had been some rough times in his life when he had felt his deceased father's presence giving him strength; maybe he could do the same for his own children. Donald's larger context was simply the fact that he believed there *was* one, more mysterious than he could define, but which held his life and would continue to do so after he died. Together we continued to explore theological and philosophical questions, catching them by the tail from time to time, finding joy and comfort in the fact that the mystery—however it is perceived—can never be fully known by the human mind. As the cancer overwhelmed his internal organs he became too weak to receive anyone outside the family except me. As sick as he was, he still wanted to explore theological possibilities.

Donald never expressed fear of death, only curiosity about it. Our verbal explorations included laughter and hope as well as tears over what he was leaving behind. This dynamic man, with his curious mind and searching heart, was vitally alive until his last conscious breath. When he died it was a peaceful death at home in the arms of his wife and children and me.

One ninety-year-old woman looks on her death as "a step in development." She has believed in reincarnation for decades, and says "It's a good working hypothesis until something better comes along." Her larger context enables her to face her death with curiosity and equanimity.

It is through curiosity and searching that our world grows large enough to fascinate us, keeping our own lives in perspective and shedding light on our larger context.

The mystery of physicists' theoretical quarks, with their exotic names—"up" and "down" and "truth" and "beauty"—excited me so much that I once preached a sermon about them. There are theories now of even smaller units of matter named mesons and bosons and more that are beyond the realm of my understanding. Some scientists speculate that matter is made up of units of consciousness. What if each of those units is something like an electron? The electron, an elementary particle that is a fundamental constituent of matter, is always spinning and is never destroyed. In my own pondering these days, I like to play with the idea that my life is a choreography of electrons that came together to create me. When I die and they are no longer needed to be the creation that I have been, maybe they'll go back out into the universe to become part of some other form or forms of life. I wonder, will my life have put a unique spin on these electrons, changed them in some small way? Can I be instrumental in their carrying a little more love and wisdom so that whatever or whoever they become part of next will benefit from the life I have lived? I don't know, but I hope so.

It's imperative that we keep pushing the outer limits of our understanding. For ongoing expansion of our inner selves and spiritual growth we must build open-ended curiosity and exploration into our responses to life. Our society cries out for concrete, black-and-white answers, longing for more simple times when our physical survival often demanded those kinds of judgments. But black-and-white thinking can't acknowledge the complexity of events. When we are overwhelmed by the moral dilemmas presented by modern life or are suffering the worst of losses, we may find ourselves in unfathomable gray areas in which there are no clear answers. But if we can find and be attentive to the quiet place within us, we may sense the presence of mystery or larger context in the midst of chaos—a context that holds all possibilities.

My first distinct memory of what I am naming "the mystery" occurred when I was six years old, living in the wilds of central Washington state, miles from any neighbors. In the dead of that particular winter there was twelve feet of snow on the ground. Thawing and freezing had left a crust that supported my small weight. The highest bar of my swing set was only two inches off the "ground," and I felt like a giant when I stepped carefully over previously airborne power lines. One night I stood silently at the edge of the forest. I'd been playing outside alone all afternoon and into evening. There was a howling loneliness inside me, yet I kept putting off going home. Under twelve feet of snow my house was only a peaked roof with a glow of light around the edges and around the hole at the front door where my father had shoveled steps from the stoop to the top of the snow. I wanted to be warm and dry but could not bring myself to go inside. The shards of angry words and hard silences that filled the small building severed any possibility of comfort and had long since drained the arteries of love.

As I stood there in the deepening darkness, huge flakes of snow began to float lazily from the black sky—they were large polka dots on the silhouettes of the tall evergreen trees. There was not a whisper of sound. The peace and silence were huge and booming, blossoming in my cells, and suddenly I felt opened up, touched, as if by the finger of a god or a magic wand, and love flooded through my being, pinning me to the snow, stunned and speechless.

Thirty years later, as an unhappy wife in a lifeless marriage, I sat alone in the backyard on a warm summer night. My husband and children had been asleep for hours. I sat through those dark hours in the lawn chair wondering if I had any options, if there was any more to life than this. Suddenly, with no warning, something totally inexplicable happened that left me weeping with hope and gratitude. It felt as if a blanket of love had wrapped completely around me, permeating my whole being with warmth. It may have lasted a split second or for several minutes—the event itself was timeless. And it changed everything. In my worst periods of life since then, when it has felt as if nothing matters and nothing more exists, the memory of that experience has reminded me that there is indeed more to life, whether or not I am able at that moment to perceive it.

An older woman shared with me her experience of being very ill and suffering through sleepless nights. One night her breathing was so labored that she sat propped up in bed for hours, thinking silently, "Okay, God, everyone else seems to believe in you, senseless as it seems. If there really is something to it, how about letting me know?" Nothing happened for a long time, so eventually she gave up. "Then," she said, "the oddest thing happened. There came a feeling of absolute clarity— no thoughts, no images, no sound, no words. I *knew,* not believed, *knew* that I was connected to everyone and everything in the universe, a total oneness with all things animate and even inanimate. It seemed that a whole new sense—other than the usual five—had opened up. I glimpsed a reality beyond any I had ever known. At that moment I didn't particularly care whether I lived or died. Any fear of death was totally wiped out. I don't know how long this feeling lasted. For those minutes (hours?), space and time both existed and did not exist. I wasn't reaching for this experience—I didn't know it existed. It completely surprised me. That indescribable event, that was both outside and inside of me, became the core of my being that is connected directly to the core of being in every other human body. This secret knowledge got me through some bad times, although it didn't keep bad things from happening. I must admit that the effects of the experience have faded with time, but I can't deny that something tremendous happened and that there were permanent changes. I still carry inside of me a sense—in spite of all the stupid things we humans do—of the rightness of things at their core."[13]

These experiences of love and clarity are a mystery to me as to the how, when, and why of them. I've often prayed—begged—for such an experience or sign and received none. If you find yourself desperate for an answer that will ease the pain of something awful that's happened to you and no signs or comfort are forthcoming, then by all means seek emotional support from trusted friends and/or professionals. If your issues include spiritual questions about meaning and you seek professional support, look for a psychotherapist who is open-minded about the human spirit and not afraid to explore these frontiers with you.

In my work as a clergywoman, chaplain, and counselor, I have met people whose lives were changed—some say transformed—by a "near-death experience." This phenomenon has stirred up much controversy among scientists. Some medical and science professionals believe that something mystical or inexplicable *can* take place. Others say that any experiences of this kind have a biological explanation and have nothing to do with life after death. But I do know of one instance of a form of life after death, which happened in a family I was intimately connected with. The couple are both deceased now, but their daughter has given me permission to tell the story using their real names.

Owen and Muriel Pearce fell in love and married in 1920. He was an engineer, she was a homemaker. Owen was successful in his vocation, but he is remembered best for his love of rhododendrons. Over time he became known as an expert with the plant, writing a monthly column for a national gardening magazine and gaining a national reputation. Owen developed a new hybrid rhododendron and named it for his wife—the "Muriel Pearce"—and planted it near their front door. For the next twenty-five years the "Muriel Pearce" bloomed like clockwork each spring, marking another year together. Owen was with Muriel when she died a few days before Christmas in the fifty-sixth year of their marriage. He phoned their minister from the nursing home and made arrangements for her funeral. When the heartbroken Owen finally arrived home, he was stunned to see one bright cluster of blossoms greeting him from the "Muriel Pearce" rhododendron. It had not been there when he'd left early that morning for the nursing home. It was the only time, before or since, that the tree produced flowers in December. That gift of love, however it happened, was the sole adornment on the church's altar the following Sunday.

There are many who believe in a literal heaven or hell and probably as many who don't. It's in our nature to be curious about the nature of life and what is going to happen to us. If there is a higher power, I expect it or she or he is secure enough to enjoy our muddling attempts to stretch our minds and hearts so that our perceptions can expand—including, especially, in those times when we stumble and curse.

Don't feel slighted if you haven't had a spiritual revelation. The ones mentioned above came to people who were struggling to be alive. You may not need a startling, life-changing experience if you have always been blessed with love and acceptance. Know that in some very important ways you are freer to engage with life because you don't carry the burden of sorrow and pain others may have.

We are surrounded by cues that point us to a bigger picture, one as large as humanity or larger than the known universe. Whatever the scale of our personal larger context, there will always be powerful parts of it that are unknowable and impossible to explain. Physicists tell us that we perceive only three or four of at least ten dimensions; a competing theory says that there are twenty-six dimensions, all of them connected. If any theory of this kind is true, then it is apparent that we are limited not only by having just five senses but also by our imaginations, especially when we don't allow them to move beyond the dictates of our biology.

In contemporary society we tend to identify with our homes, roles, and titles, sometimes even with our furniture and the pictures on our walls. Someday many of us will have to give up possessions in order to receive the physical care required for a chronic illness or disability. We will be seriously traumatized by these changes if we have never identified ourselves as part of anything larger and more meaningful than our roles and possessions.

I think of Manny, an intelligent man whose accomplishments included having designed and built his own home decades earlier. The home was so outstanding, both in design and craftsmanship, that it had been featured in a large metropolitan newspaper. Over the decades his children grew to adulthood and his wife died, and eventually his own physical decline made it impossible for him to maintain the house. Finally, unable to care for himself, he moved into a lovely private apartment in a nearby assisted-living facility where staff members (as well as several of the resident widows) showered him with attention and support. His children all worked full-time, but at least one of them visited him every day. But Manny was miserable. He had only one definition of home, and that was the house he had built. When I saw him, his statement was always the same: "I need someone to tell me what I have to do to get back home." Manny's children tried hard to make things better for their dad. In the beginning they took him back to the house at least once a week so he could see that it was still there and part of the family. But the property taxes were becoming a burden, now that they were putting their own children through college. Afraid that they would soon need to sell the house, they began to work evenings and weekends to repair the years of neglect (he hadn't allowed them to help him while he lived in the house). Meanwhile, Manny's physical and mental decline continued while he still asked everyone how he could get back home.

Manny was never able to appreciate the comfortable surroundings to which he had moved or the support, attention, and love he received and needed from family, other residents, and staff. If Manny had had a bigger picture of life, he might have been able to grieve the loss of his home until he could finally let go of it. He might have reconciled himself to the fact that the time comes when we all have to let go of how things were, and look for the pleasure and meaning in what is left. But Manny was never able to conceive of any kind of meaningful life outside of his beloved house. Emotionally, he was homeless when he died.

I believe we are all born with the inherent ability to sense something beyond what we can see, measure, understand, or know with the intellect. Giving it the name of a god is a way of personifying and remembering this larger dimension. Many represent it with symbol and ritual, in much the same way that we honor the birthdays and anniversaries of those we care about or hang photographs of distant loved ones to keep their presence near us.

Scientists who study the intricacies of biology, of ecosystems, of weather, of physics, may or may not think in terms of a larger context—but the wondrous workings and mysteries of their subject keep them as dedicated as priests. People who load their cars with skis or fishing poles and camping gear, who put their mountain bikes on car racks or their ropes and carabiners in the trunk, who don their hiking boots and fill their water bottles on weekends, are leaving behind the everyday world of commerce to reconnect with nature and its implications of a vastness both bigger and more intricate than our daily vision allows us. The busy professional, homemaker, or retiree who with a jolt looks up from his or her communion with dirt, bugs, and weeds and realizes that it has grown too dark to garden anymore was probably lost for a while in spirituality—a sense of connection to something bigger than daily routines. Parents and grandparents who hold a newborn child and weep for joy have touched the heart of a larger context. When the song of the robin or the view from the top of the ski slope causes you to catch your breath, it's probably because you are experiencing the reality of things unseen and more powerful than the routine of your daily life. Many people find it in the music, the ritual, the grandness or simplicity of their religious practice.

Once we find and experience our larger context, we can open ourselves to the possibilities it holds and grow into an understanding of the vital part of it that we are, no matter what stage of life or physical and mental shape we may be in.

When we have discovered and internalized a larger context, one that is our spiritual "home," our living itself can become an expression of it.

Remember, to find these principles, one of the things we must develop is a capacity for exploration, a searching for meanings and connections. The search itself is crucial. If you are not asking hard questions of life, if you are not carefully testing what others tell you, then you are not engaged with all the potential aspects of your own unique and wonderful life.

# 7

# Develop a Philosophy or Theology of Receiving

Mavis Stendle's nursing home room glowed in the afternoon, the sunlight reflecting off the soft pink of her furnishings, her favorite color. Diffused by sheer curtains, the light created a fittingly warm background for her open and gentle heart. Mavis, as short as she was round, was racked with the pain of severe arthritis, and in recent years episodes of cardiac arrest had sent her to the hospital several times. With her failing heart and her mobility severely limited by the arthritis, she had made her last move, to the nursing home, two years earlier. Mavis's gentle presence and dry humor had made her a favorite with everyone through all of these crises and changes. The nursing home staff loved being with her and made extra stops at her room to see if there was anything she needed. Feeling welcomed and validated by her presence and genuine interest, they confided their troubles to her, shared stories about their children, their lovers, their spouses, their holiday plans. Mavis received the most and best attention on her floor.

I dropped in weekly, but the content of our visits was different. She told me what she didn't want the others to know.

Behind her hospitable nature and warm smile she hid the demoralizing belief that she was not only useless, but a burden as well. "I can't do anything for anybody," she told me week after week. "I don't know why I'm still alive!" A lifelong devoted church member, Mavis had lived by the value that it's better to give than to receive. Now unable to do or give in the ways that were familiar to her, she was haunted by the awful suspicion that God, in allowing her to live past her usefulness, had abandoned her.

Mavis died four years after moving into the nursing home, years during which she felt worthless, powerless, burdensome, and betrayed by her God. Despite all the evidence, she was never able to comprehend the fact that she was anything but burdensome—she made people laugh, she made them feel valuable and important. With her assumption of what "giving" meant, she had not been able to see that her genuine interest in and love for people uplifted everyone who came in contact with her. Her understanding of what constituted giving came from her years of activity in the church's programs for helping others. She could not see that what she gave by just being herself was priceless to those of us privileged to be around her. Years after her death, the staff still speak of her with gratitude and affection.

The ethic "It's better to give than to receive" permeates our society, whether or not we follow its instruction. It is a fine value to live by; the problem is that our definition of giving is too narrow. People tend to think giving means doing. We are good at this kind of giving. But how about the many gifts one can contribute through simple kindness, through just being oneself?

Giving by doing makes us feel good, it makes us feel valuable. Serving food in a soup kitchen, volunteering at a hospital, taking meals to a sick friend—these are their own reward. For those who have made these activities a big part of their lives, even basing their sense of self-worth on doing these things, the idea that someday they will no longer be able to do them is unthinkable. Experiencing the physical limitations of our last years can be devastating when helping others has been a guiding value. When I suggest to disabled or ill elders that giving takes many forms and that opportunities to give are still available to them, not many are able to believe it. Most never shake the feeling that as elders constrained by physical limitations they are of no value. The financial problems many disabled elders experience only add to their sense of being a burden to their families and to society.

In my work with chronically ill elders I learned that the emotional and spiritual ability to receive is *essential* to maintaining any sense of dignity and self in old age. A woman in her eighties told me: "The most important thing in our whole lives is just this—each other. It doesn't matter which end of the bond you are on—and, with all due respect to Jesus, I maintain that it is more generous to receive than it is to give! Everybody loves to give, but nobody wants to accept. What I'm saying is that there is beauty in acceptance. As long as you're young and strong, you love to serve people who are older and weaker than you, or if anyone is in trouble, you rush to help them. That comes naturally. What does not come naturally and must be learned is how to accept. When people assist you, you must enjoy it too, and that isn't so easy. Feel the pleasure of the giver and respond to it; accept the help people offer you with joy. That is what true gratitude is—joy. Make it pleasant for those who give so they won't resent you. Start right now accepting little favors that you don't really need. If you practice this with real joy, you will add color and depth to your life."[14]

Social workers who do research with elders say it's a crucial transition in late life to acknowledge our need for help and to ask for it. They call this "mature dependence." The meaning of the word "mature" is "full development." Learning to receive is part of our growth into completion.

Those of you raised in families that gave freely and joyfully may have a relatively easy time receiving help—you learned early to sense the caring attitude of the giver. Even so, make sure that the quest to make a place for yourself in the world as an adult hasn't led you into judging your self-worth based on what you are able to do rather than on who you are. If you were raised in a family that gave little, if anything, without attaching strings, you will find being on the receiving end almost impossible unless you concentrate on the issue intently and start practicing now.

Despite what I've learned while working with ill and disabled elders, for me receiving is still a seriously underdeveloped skill. I've spent my own life refusing help and not even thinking of asking for it. I'm proud of my self-sufficiency, but sometimes it comes with a very high price. This is a legacy of the way I was raised, my own strong will, and flashbacks to memories of being in need when I was a child.

Many members of my family have suffered from biologically based depression exacerbated by hard circumstances. My parents survived severe difficulties in their own childhoods and were so much in need of love, nurture, and support themselves that they had few emotional resources to deal with the needs of a child. I was a main target for their frustration, grief, and rage. Never knowing what to expect, I was always afraid of them. If I didn't do something "right"—and "right" was a moving target—my parents' impatience turned to rage that ridiculed, physically punished, and shamed me for my efforts. To avoid humiliation, I learned not to ask for anything, especially help. I was emotionally isolated with no one to help me figure things out. I learned to accomplish tasks on my own and, preferably, unobserved.

The result of living with constant fear was that I developed a condition known as post-traumatic stress syndrome, which, like depression, is biologically based. Stress chemicals flood the body, including the brain, long enough that one's physiology reacts automatically to stimuli that are reminiscent of the original trauma. A smell, a sound, colors, even lighting that is similar to that which was present during the trauma can cause one to experience the old feelings of anxiety or despair. Even now I sometimes feel the old anxiety when offered help. These feelings are so uncomfortable that my kneejerk reaction is usually "No, thank you."

This automatic rejection of help cost me plenty several years ago when I slipped into a depressive episode through a combination of working too hard, skipping meals, and not getting enough rest. I had felt it coming on—with my genetic inheritance, I had experienced depression before—but my regular doctor was on leave and I didn't want to risk seeing a new one. And part of me wanted to prove that I could overcome this by myself. I toughed it out for a month of anguish and despair that seriously disabled me.

Depression symptoms widely vary, but mine have always included feeling as if a heavy lead blanket has been dropped over my body and wrapped around my brain. My limbs become so heavy that all movement feels as if it's taking place in deep water. My mind with its leaden burden can't concentrate or think clearly. Creativity flies out the window. Since many of us who experience this affliction have learned to put on a good front, dragging ourselves out of bed and back into the mainstream every day, most people don't know how badly off we are at these times.

When this particular depressive episode hit, I was working on a huge project for which I had great passion. The work came to a halt as I sat and stared blankly at it every day, weeping with frustration because I couldn't concentrate on the outlines and ideas I'd created. I was by turns angry, anxious, and grieving, while completely devoid of energy. Still I waited, determined to get through this on my own.

After a month of being stuck in this mire, I was talked into phoning my HMO by an insistent friend. When I finally called, the response was immediate: I was scheduled to see a physician the following morning; copious lab tests were ordered, and the next day I was in the office of a specialist in brain chemistry. This rapid response was far beyond what I'd expected. They understood that this was a physical illness that needed immediate treatment. The lab tests revealed that the dosage of a prescribed medication was too high. Within two days of my initial phone call, the dose was cut back and a new medication introduced.

It took another three months for me to get back to my usual level of functioning. Altogether I'd lost four months' work on a project that was not only my passion but my livelihood. My HMO came through in full force to provide the assistance I needed.[15]

Depression had been only part of the problem. The main stumbling block was my pride. If I had not insisted on toughing it out for so long to prove I didn't need anyone's help, in spite of the fact that I was paying insurance premiums for the services, I could have saved myself a lot of suffering and lost time.

Obviously, asking for help doesn't apply only to depression. I've met many widows and widowers who had tried unsuccessfully to convince their sick spouse to see a doctor. By the time the husband or wife finally made an appointment, his or her heart, lung, kidney, or liver disease or cancer was so advanced that recovery was impossible.

Here's a passage from my journal during that bout with depression: "What is the alternative to depression and suicide —resignation? withdrawal? bitterness? It's surrender. I don't know what will happen in the next few minutes, much less the coming months. Surrender into the moment. In this moment I am having trouble breathing. Concentrate on my breath. In surrender I find myself weeping tears of frustration and grief that this breathing is all I can do—that my day is not seamless with competence and plans, ideas, creativity, and the pure joy of having a body. Now I stutter through the moments, terrified of the despair that can freeze my heart and mind at any moment. Surrender is an action I must choose over bitterness. It's not giving up or giving in—it's a giving over. Surrender does not include withdrawal."

Surrender is an attitude I had to consciously choose over anger, frustration, and bitterness. Surrender carries within it the seeds of trust—trust in myself to survive and to get the assistance I need, trust in a network of professionals and friends who genuinely care about me. With other physical setbacks that may overtake me as I come to my last years, I want to remember the importance of getting through the next moment, even if its only activity is breathing. In these experiences of surrender I have discovered that most of the time I can and do believe that the universe and my small part in it will unfold as they should. This knowledge helps me let go and live in the moment. This is a small part of my own particular path of surrendering to what I cannot change and, most important, accepting help. I keep learning the hard way that toughing it out carries a high price in poor health, lost time, and crushed self-esteem.

It's normal to have good days and bad days—days when our spirits, emotions, and energy are high and joyful, and difficult days when we are down. In these latter times it's important that we learn to give to ourselves. To be helpful in our last years, any philosophy or theology of receiving must also include the ability to be kind to ourselves.

Certainly in your last years you will continue to perform the tasks and self-care that you are able to do, but you will learn that impairments may have made impossible the schedule of tasks you were able to carry out even a few short months before. You will have relatively good days when you have the energy and stamina to attend to the activities that are important to you. You will also have days in which your energy is so low that getting dressed may be beyond your powers or interest. On those days, eating a little food may be all you can handle. To scold or disparage yourself is counterproductive. You may already feel frustration and grief over your limitations; the last thing you need is your own unkindness, which will only make you feel worse than you already do.

Beginning now, pay attention to what issues arise within you when you are offered help. Does it raise feelings of obligation, threatening your need to be in control? Does it feel like a blow to your pride? If we are disabled, we may find ourselves resenting the person who is doing for us what we can't do for ourselves. For those who are on the receiving end, there may be the fear that what the giver is giving can also be taken away by whim or circumstance. We may feel shame that the other has so much to give us and we have so little to give back. Any of these feelings are painful and may be too uncomfortable to live with if we do not prepare ourselves to live graciously with receiving.

Receiving can be especially difficult for those whose work is providing care to others. Many of us know giving as our main way to receive respect, love, and acceptance and to feel valuable. Being forced by circumstances to accept help from others turns our identity and self-perceptions inside out. People are often amused to find that many physicians, when they are on the receiving end of care, are difficult patients. Physicians are no different from anyone else in the helping professions—they may simply not have the skill or knowledge about how to receive.

Your understanding of receiving may be in religious or secular language. The most important thing is that you have thought about your definition of being on the receiving end, applied it, refined it when necessary, and found it to be practical and supportive of you when you require assistance of any kind.

In Botswana, the Herero people take care of their elders with pride. It's the old ones who are in charge of the care and teaching of village children, whether or not they are related. People of all ages in the village consider caring for their elders a responsibility, and doing so is a source of pride and prestige, not a burden. The Herero elders accept care as a confirmation of their lifelong interdependence with others.[16] The Herero know what we don't—that none of us is ever really independent. Too often in Western society, when we speak of someone who requires care we are locking that person into a role that will soon come to define him or her. If you're on the receiving end and being defined as dependent—especially when you are old—people tend to forget the whole of you. They forget that you have survived and given much in the process; they forget the hard work and effort you put into living. It becomes easier for people to depersonalize and devalue you, treat you like a child. These assumptions on the part of others ignore the fact that we are always interdependent with one another.

Western contemporary society does not value its elders or give them a status they can be proud of. But people develop and grow only in interaction with each other. Dependence and independence form a continuum, and where we are along that continuum changes as we move through the stages of our life. Dependence is as normal as independence, it's just a different place on the continuum of interdependence. When we become elders, if we have physical and/or mental limitations, we may be able to "do" less, but we can—with preparation and skill—"be" more. Being who we are, if we have done our homework toward completion, is a priceless legacy we can leave with those who care for us and love us.

You must, of course, respect your limits, especially in late life. There will be days when you are too run-down to reach out to anyone. If you are at home, build in as much rest as you can—preferably the whole day. If you're living in a care institution, ask your care providers to put a sign on your door that says "Please Do Not Disturb," and turn off your telephone. You may need to stay in a fetal position or something akin to that until your strength rallies enough that you feel up to interacting with others. If your care providers, whoever they may be and whatever the setting is in which they care for you, do not respect your wishes, don't hesitate to ask a friend to advocate for you. Confrontation of any kind is stressful, and when you are old, it may present itself to you at a time when you have little energy. If you have learned how to be your own friend, you won't hesitate to stand up for yourself by learning what recourse is available to you and asking someone else to be your advocate when you are not able to advocate for yourself.

In 1978, under the Older Americans Act, the federal government established the Long-Term Care Ombudsman Program. Every state is required to provide ombudspersons to advocate for those in institutional care settings. Each facility is required to post the phone number of the assigned ombudsperson in a place where all residents can see it. Information can also be acquired by phoning your Area Agency on Aging listed in the United States Government section of the phone book. You can phone and request a visit from your ombudsman, who will negotiate with the facility or the family for what you need.

The ombudsman I worked with was a retired social worker. He was good at conflict resolution and clear communication. When we suspected that one of our nursing home residents was being used by a doctor at a local hospital for experimental drugs without her permission, I called our ombudsman to meet with our staff. We formed a team to create a safety net around the resident. Our social worker phoned the hospital, telling them of our concern and explaining that one of us would be with our resident each remaining day of her stay there. The ombudsman was part of that visiting team and continued to follow up with the patient after she'd left the hospital and come back to us.

Sadly, when we are beyond the stages of robust health, it often is the case that our basic rights are no longer respected, despite federal law. For some reason this fact is more acceptable in institutions than it is in family homes. For example, you may have always been a night person, but the institution may assign you to a room at the end of the hall where the nurse's aide begins first to put her patients to bed. Never asleep before midnight, you now find yourself in bed at 7:00 P.M. Or let's say you like to sleep late and have breakfast around 11:00, or no breakfast at all. When you are in a care institution, you may find your breakfast tray put in front of you at 7:30 A.M. whether you want it or not. If you don't eat it, a notation is made in your medical record. If you complain about the early hour, an aide in a bad mood may write you up as uncooperative. Care settings are getting better, but there is a lot of room for improvement, especially in their philosophical and functional attitudes about their clients' individuality and rights. As you enter your old age, if you need care from others, don't forget that legally *you do not lose your civil liberties,* but you may have to fight for them.

The training of both the heart and the mind to adjust to and accept being cared for is foundational to a workable philosophy or theology of receiving. Like the other skills and attributes needed for us to grow into completion, this one also takes practice to develop, beginning with the baby steps of loss in middle age when we are at the peak of our power and energy and therefore less likely to be threatened by offers of help or gifts of service.

For most people, receiving is hard work, and if we're not prepared for it, our responses will range from rage to shame to withdrawal and depression. One nursing home resident who had been struggling with the issue of her dependence finally had a breakthrough that allowed her to accept graciously and genuinely the help of others. Always an avid reader, she had that day been brought a dictionary by the facility's librarian, who had told her she could keep it as long as she wanted to. Other staff members had been constantly bringing her small gifts of chocolate, flowers from their gardens, even a bottle of wine and a stemmed glass (having gotten the physician's permission). Because she had been so independent all of her life, never asking for help, she had not known how to receive all the kindness shown her. But that day, the dictionary she had wanted for so long (but hadn't asked for) was the catalyst for her realization that the people she was dependent on really cared about her well-being. She was weeping when I dropped in to see her. Through her tears she told me that that gesture of the dictionary had finally broken her open to see the oneness of us all.

It's a big shift from being able to "do" things to merely "being." "Doing" changes things; "being" sees what's happening and acknowledges reality, honoring the good parts and deciding what, if anything, can be done about the bad parts. "Being" accepts. Receiving and noticing "what is," including the person who is assisting you, does make a big difference. However serious your limitations may be, if you have this insight, you will still have the option of caring, of sharing laughter and tears, a moment of tenderness, respect, affection. It's impossible to measure what a difference these gifts make in the lives of those who care for us, whether they are professionals, family, or friends. These are things they cannot buy at any price.

Receiving is honorable. If it weren't for receivers there could be no givers. Receiving is sacred. It recognizes the spirit of the gift or service, whether or not the person is being paid to do it. Being open to receive is holy work because it's an act of trust and letting go, allowing the giver to receive the blessing of giving. If it is more blessed to give than to receive, then the receiver is the bestower of the blessing.

To be sacred, the giving and the receiving must come from a part of us that knows we are all connected and we each have something to offer the other. Giving and receiving are opposite sides of the same coin. Receiving entails trust in our own value and our having respect for the giver. By receiving we reinforce the giver and are ourselves supported and affirmed by the gift. In this way we participate in life's goodness and assist in its flourishing. There are times in our lives when the only way we can give back is to receive.

# 8

# A Life Complete

There are immediate benefits associated with preparing emotionally and spiritually for your last stage of life. You have probably already noticed that each of the skills and issues raised in the foregoing chapters requires a type of attention and thoughtfulness we don't often indulge in in our busy lives. These preparations, whether they are in the emotional or the spiritual section of this book, are all spiritual practices in that they will bring you closer to the essence of your life. They may move you into previously hidden grief through the awareness of what you have already lost. They may uncover anticipatory grief over what you will eventually lose as you grow closer to the end of your life. But they will also carry you through your grief, opening your eyes to recognize your part in the larger picture of life and the precious nature of so much we don't ordinarily notice. Thinking of the pain of delving into the hidden and sore corners of our inner selves, I remember the line of a song: "I could have missed the pain, but I would have had to miss the dance."[17] That's exactly what I don't want you to do—miss the dance that is your own life.

When this book was in its embryonic stages, I discussed its developing content each month with a group of thirty to fifty residents of the retirement center. During one of these meetings a participant commented, "If we're lucky, we develop the humor, love, joy, and humility to discover life again—as a child. That is wisdom, and it usually takes old age to find it."

The word "completion" generally refers to something that has reached its fulfillment or its conclusion—all parts are whole and entire, having reached full development. And so it can be that in our living we move toward our own completion through a gradual unfolding—the working out of the details of the self. One might say that the goal of life is the Universal—your effect on it, your concern for it, and your involvement with what I've referred to as a larger context.

Old age, when we are emotionally and spiritually prepared for it, is the last step and opportunity to achieve full development and fulfillment before we die. One nursing home resident described completion as "a very powerful feeling that has no form, so I can't really talk about it. But for the first time I realize that I am a small part of all humanity and that this *is* the meaning of being alive!" She went on to say that "our culture sees dependent late life, especially in a nursing home, as warehousing and isolation from life. My experience living with severe physical limitations has moved me *into* life, as one with life, more than ever before!" Another elder said he had "let go of everything, except the values that are eternal." Neither of these people claimed to be religious in any formal sense.

Completion is a feeling the individual has, and each person's experience of it will be unique—no one else lives in your skin or has walked your particular life path. Nobody else's concept of completion should become a standard by which others judge us—or, worse, diagnose us.

Disabled and chronically ill elders I've known who have achieved completion have a quality about them that is exciting, interesting, and energizing. I am so grateful that I have met and talked with many of them to ask them what their experience is of living with severe limitations. They report feeling a calmness, peacefulness, reconciliation, acceptance, and deeper interest in the world. Generally there is no fear of death among these people: most are simply curious about what it's going to be like. Instead they are awed by the quality and depth of their relationships, their emotions and spirituality. They are curious about things they may never have thought of before. Even though they fear the possibility of unbearable pain, they are also optimistic; most of their moments contain hope about the quality of their health and the timing of their death. They view their decline and demise with a feeling of "rightness" about being part of the natural cycle of life.

Ninety-eight-year-old Hester lived next door to her best friend. Every evening after dinner they took turns meeting in one apartment or the other for a little brandy or sherry. One evening Hester announced to her friend, "Anticipating my demise, I gave my wedding ring to my daughter today." Hester, having outfoxed the intentions of medical opinion, had released herself twice from the nursing home and was able to live for another year and a half in her own apartment with part-time home health aides and family support before she quietly died one night while preparing for bed. She had been planning for her death for several years, prefacing many of her statements with "Anticipating my demise . . ."

The Akan people of Ghana say that "the rainbow of death encircles everyone's neck" and that "everyone will have to climb the ladder of death someday." Imagine living each day aware of a rainbow wrapped around us like a mantle or vestment that affirms the sacredness of our lives, or thinking of death as a climb to greater heights than we have been to before, an event to anticipate rather than fear! The knowledge of one's mortality is built into the consciousness of many indigenous and tribal people. Many of them, separated from much influence (so far) of Western cultures, live with the awareness of their part in the larger scheme of things, including the ongoing life of the tribe and the preciousness of their environment. Moving in harmony with the cycles of nature, they are more likely to "live" than merely "exist." Seldom do they work the long hours demanded by Western commerce. For them, death is part of the natural order and has its own purpose. Some see it as a gift at the end of a long life, and a gift to upcoming generations—a moving out of the space one has occupied to make room for new life. There are concrete expressions of some dimensions of death. The Parsi people in India leave their deceased one's body on a high scaffold as food for the birds. A Venezuelan tribe drinks the ashes of the cremated body so the deceased will remain a member of the tribe. For many of these people, death is not an "ending" but a "becoming"—a return to nature from which they came. In their wait in the ice and snow, the wilderness, the desert, the jungle, they make the sacred commitment of becoming One with nature again, a transition that merely includes death.

In Western society, we have traded "becoming" for the most expensive and extravagant maintenance in history. Instead of moving toward "becoming," most of us perceive only "ending." I've often wondered if this is why death comes so slowly to so many who desperately want it.

The treasures of late life are not apparent to us when we are young. Only the heart and mind seasoned by years of observation and engagement allow us the discernment of humor, love, beauty, gentleness, and the presence of the sacred embedded in life. It is this wise heart-mind combination that continues to discover our worth and the deeper meanings of life into our last years. Being able to engage in exploration of meaning and purpose in late life is the payoff of years of having practiced it and of having become our own friend. This continuing exploration allows us to move into closure and a deeper knowing of life before we die.

If we find ourselves in physically limited circumstances in old age, with life no longer structured by the demands of obligation and work, we may move into an experience of timelessness. Whether it's Monday or Saturday, the daily routine is pretty much the same, punctuated by meals, the evening news broadcast, and whatever other activities our aged bodies and minds will have the interest and energy for. To many elders these routines are not boring but are a reflection of their limited energy, offering just the right amount of daily structure. Many, in fact, find this wonderfully liberating and begin to live more with the seasons and cycles rather than with days and weeks. They report new freedom and a qualitative difference in how they experience the moments, especially a deeper appreciation for the subtleties of nature and the humor and kindness of others. The present moment is available to them as never before, because the distractions allowed and demanded by strength, good health, and obligations have been left behind. Many disabled and chronically ill elders experience this timelessness with gratitude and a sense of something sacred being present in their lives. These are the people who have learned to accept who they are and to respect and honor their needs. They also accept their decline and death as a natural part of life.

Emotionally and spiritually prepared elders will not *lose* who they *were*, but will *become* who they *are*. Having successfully achieved their whole self, these people are free to soar in their hearts and minds—to fly out to all of life, including their own present and past, with their questions, their thoughts, and their love. Many bridges will have been crossed and even burned along the way, but we can arrive at this new and unknown territory with all our accumulated skills, knowing who we have been and who we can still be. Those who meet us and provide services for us won't know much about our past; they will relate to the essence of who we have become over the years. We will have only the immediate truth of ourselves to show.

Eighty-nine-year-old Rose displayed qualities of completion. She had been a high-fashion model in the 1920s, sweeping gracefully through New York's best stores in elegant gowns, tempting customers to buy the elegance and beauty she displayed. Seventy years later she still had the grace, sophistication, and elegance demanded by that work, despite the osteoporosis that had crumbled and bent her frame like a heap of loose stones. Somehow she had managed to maintain her air of imperiousness, and she loved it when I greeted her as "the Empress."

When she could no longer care for herself and moved to the nursing home, she permitted only three of us to visit her, dictating—as she always had—what she wanted and needed. Those first months in the nursing home were pure hell for her. The facility was far too noisy, making the relaxation she desperately needed nearly impossible. She was totally dependent, even for toileting. Her lungs, crowded by her collapsing spine and ribs, could not expand enough to allow in sufficient oxygen; her breathing was strenuous and painful. The osteoporosis caused her brittle bones to break spontaneously, leaving her in searing pain with each movement. Her despair leaked out in short gasps as she struggled to tell me that she wanted to die. She knew that even as the current breaks were healing more of the same would follow. "Why can't I die? What's the point of this?" she would ask me week after week.

One day when I went to see her, I knew the moment I entered her room that something had changed. She could hardly wait to tell me that right after I'd left the week before, she had a vision of a tombstone with the words "Trust Me" engraved on it. When she saw it, she said she felt so comforted that her whole body and mind relaxed and "let go." Since then she had experienced less pain, her breathing was less labored, and she no longer worried about things, including how long it would be before she died. She asked a friend to help her catch up on her correspondence, and she managed short phone conversations. She interacted with staff members as much as she was able and otherwise lay in bed thinking or letting her mind and heart "float." I asked her if she got bored. "No," she replied, "there's too much to think about and wonder about: too many nice people to remember." She told me she now had "a powerful, active patience. It feels like it surrounds me like an aura." She added, "This patience isn't like most, a feeble virtue that is its own reward—this is like a strong magnet which draws solutions to problems."

Months later, as a hospital staff attempted yet again to straighten her deformed body on a CAT Scan table, she demanded that they stop. "Enough!" she yelled at them. She confronted her doctor until he finally agreed: she would have no more tests and take no more food, only fluids and medication to control her pain. She came back to the nursing home in very high spirits and began giving last-minute advice to all who came by to see her. "Mary," she said to her nurse's aide, shaking her finger at her, "promise me you'll lose weight—that extra fat you carry around your middle is just not healthy! If you don't lose that, I'll come back and haunt you!"

Eight days after she stopped eating, the staff said she wouldn't live through that night—it was a Tuesday—and Rose asked me to sit with her. We talked about how she would probably not see morning, certainly not her usual Friday cocktail hour. Finally she lay peacefully, eyes closed. Then she remembered two phone calls and asked me to make them. Then came hours of stillness and silence. I moved into a free-floating, relaxed trance, matching my breathing to hers. Certain that she had slipped into a coma, I was startled when she suddenly said, "This is perfect. It's exactly as I had hoped it would be." Another hour of silence, and again, "This is perfect, I am at peace."

She did live to see morning—lived another three days, in fact, dying on Friday about an hour before it would have been time for her cocktail. In those three days, weeping staff members and friends had come to say goodbye. She comforted and scolded every one of them with a few final strict words of advice, including, "Don't cry about me—I'm happy!"

Rose had entered the nursing home with a lifetime of well-honed coping skills and an open heart and mind. In the end, it was those strengths that uprighted her sinking ship and provided her emotional and spiritual quality of life. She lived and engaged with life until her last breath.

Another woman, Maxine, whose body was constantly racked with pain from an untreatable genetic physical condition, was still able to get to the retirement facility's dining room for one or two meals a day. The rest of the time she had to lie prone on her bed to avoid the stabbing pain that often made her cry out in agony. I was intrigued by the contents of a letter she wrote while in the lowest state I had ever seen her in. Here are some excerpts:

"I have not written for some time because I don't know what to say. The sad fact is that I am not doing well at all. I am barely able to care for myself and that means I will have to leave my apartment of 17 years [and move to the nursing home]. And what happens to the body and soul then? I have seen it all too often . . . and haven't cared for it at all. There are untold thousands of such warehoused in the USA and I have little taste to be one. But there is little I can do about it . . . At least I fit in well around here. We have the lame, blind, deaf and all grades between . . . They all receive better care than in most places.

"And it is spring here. Daffodils are out, plums are blooming, the Canada geese are in pairs and some days ago there was a barn swallow. Red wing blackbirds are calling. I seldom go outside but I do have a nice view of the goings on . . . and I thoroughly enjoy the blue sky and fluffy white clouds . . . Life goes on."[18]

The one thing that does not have to diminish with age is the heart. It is able to continue to expand and grow in depth and perception and understanding. An open heart has no limits; it is bigger than the body. It can be bigger than its circumstances unless intolerable physical or mental pain is untreated.

There are still too many doctors who overlook a person's complaints because the patient is old. In the case of physical pain, some doctors are afraid to prescribe sufficient medication because of the possibility that the elder would become addicted or that the medication itself might hasten death and bring about a medical malpractice suit and the loss of the physician's license. Since Oregonians passed the "Death with

Dignity" initiative in 1994, which allows physicians to aid their terminally ill patients in dying, the state has become one of the best in the nation for its success with pain control. The initiative was a grassroots effort that served as a wake-up call to legislators and medical professionals that a majority of people do not believe they should have to suffer in their dying. People whose pain is managed are more likely to choose to live for as long as they can, even—and especially—when they have the option of deciding that for themselves. With the aid-in-dying law now in effect, many physicians are relieved that they no longer have to compromise their patients' care by withholding federally regulated pain medication.

In the case of mental pain, depression is reported to be the most undertreated illness among chronically ill and disabled elders. This lack of treatment is, I believe, the direct result of ageism among medical professionals themselves. Reflecting the attitude of our society, many physicians assume that if you are old and sick, depression is normal. Consciously or unconsciously, they are personally identifying with how they believe they would feel in similar circumstances. Another problem is that few physicians have specialized training in geriatrics—the appropriate treatment of elders. All too often, drugs or combinations of drugs prescribed for the ailments commonly experienced by elders are themselves the cause of depression.

If you do everything suggested in this book but end up with untreated depression or intolerable pain, your prior efforts and preparations for these last years will be of limited help. Treatment may require medication, changes in medications you're already taking, and perhaps psychological counseling; in any event, it does require professional help. Make sure you have a doctor you can talk to who will listen. If you can find one, engage the services of a geriatrician, a physician whose specialty is geriatrics. Since our body's systems change as we age, our medical professionals should have expertise about how to work with those changes. Regarding depression and physical pain you *must* be prepared—you personally, your ombudsman, or someone close to you—to be militant in seeing that you receive the treatment you need. As I explained in earlier chapters, acknowledging your personal truth, caring for yourself, and getting the help you need is a form of self-respect that recognizes that you, your well-being, and your quality of life are important for as long as you live.

Those who are coming close to completion will prepare for death as they would for a long trip to an unknown place. They will leave their house in order, and they will have said their goodbyes. But in the case of death, instead of packing they will have been spending a long time unpacking. One person who survived a near-death experience, saying that she traveled to a life beyond, reported that all we get to take with us is our love and our knowledge. I find this thought comforting, for what else about our lives could be more important than these?

Waiting for death is like being in any waiting room. It's usually uncomfortable, the magazines are at least one or two years old, and sometimes you're there a lot longer than you expected. Say, for instance, you've arrived at your airport but all the planes are tied up in Chicago due to snow. You still have choices. You can sit around peeved and grumbling. You can withdraw from everything that's going on around you. Or you can let go of the outcome and enjoy this time of no responsibilities, watching and engaging with those you meet. Some people arrive so unprepared for this, the last trip of their lives, that they have not closed their house, stopped the paper, said goodbye, or left instructions. Instead they arrive at the airport burdened with the baggage of their lives, unable to be in the present moment and too disoriented and frantic to hug those who have come to see them off. Unprepared, they are not able to say goodbye or think clearly about the trip ahead.

But death will come eventually, and as we wait, we can listen to our internal truth for anything left unfinished. In anticipating our leaving we can also continue to look for opportunities to love, appreciate, and to encourage. I believe that our task, up to our last breath, is to encourage and to love.

Eda LeShan has written, "The most serene deaths, when they come, are to people who have no unfinished business."[19] Perhaps we, too, can earn one of the greatest phrases of respect I've heard: Elie Wiesel said of his grandfather that he was "the man whose presence had sanctified a small piece of the universe."[20] A lifetime is a work of art, a statement of perseverance and creativity, and most of all, a statement of courage. These last, physically limited years, if we are prepared for them, are holy ground.

I have written this book because the majority of elders I've known have spent their last years in depression, despair, hostility, fear, or numbness because they have been unprepared for the reality of life ending. Their experience of this crucial developmental stage is a surreal nightmare that can last for years. But I've also seen severely ill and disabled elders who have had a completely different experience, one stimulated by affection, love, curiosity, patience, and interest in all things around them. These people have reached full development of self on the level of emotions and spirit, often long before they die. The time they have left is a bonus of freedom to love, engage, and explore the life both inside and outside of them. I have written this book because my own peers, afraid and lacking any constructive ways to think about it, tend to ignore their long-distance future. Avoiding knowledge of the rainbow that encircles them, they miss the preciousness of their days and themselves.

It is my hope that this material will help bring hope and purpose to the rest of your life, that you will be able to anticipate your final years with less fear, recognizing them as an accomplishment. Like all marathon runners, you'll take the appropriate routes and move as skillfully as you can around curves and up and down hills when you have the route and the finish line in mind. You may "hit the wall," what athletes describe as feeling they can't move another step, but when you have the skills in place you can continue on, making it to the finish line exhausted but exuberant over what you've completed.

Running a long race is not easy. You may get shin splints, as I still do when it comes to receiving. But remember that you are to do this work as your own best friend. Remorse may be appropriate at times, but if you accept the limitations of your knowledge at the time you erred, you will be able to move through the remorse. This will allow you to be more knowledgeable about what choices to make in the future. Processing what is true for us in this way frees our hearts and minds for the laughter, joy, and tears of the moment, unencumbered by past mistakes.

Practice being acutely aware of your interdependence for all that you have and do. Along with all the bad, the world is full of people who go out of their way to make a positive difference. You may already be one of them. Remember, you *always* make a difference. You get to decide if your difference will enhance or negate life.

Plan with your last years in mind, including the fact that you may be ill or disabled for some time. That, too, will be a developmental stage, with challenges that will help you add the finishing touches to your life. This is the time when we learn things we couldn't have learned earlier, the time when we gain deeper wisdom about ourselves and the whole of life. Those who are completed appear to cross the finish line of death with peace and satisfaction. One dying elder's last communication was to his wife: he winked, he smiled, and giving a "thumbs up" signal, he died.

Whether or not death is the end of us, our leaving this plane of existence is timely and right. The next generation needs the experience of being the elders, the matriarchs and patriarchs. It's their turn to be the teachers of wisdom for younger generations so they in turn can grow in depth and wisdom and one day take their place as the elders.

To those who have died, who have finished this joyful and heartbreaking race called life, we should say, "Congratulations! You did it!" Hooray to each of us as we make the finish line! Our lifetimes are the longest and most difficult race of all. If we are paying attention to our needs, if we are practicing and conditioning ourselves, listening for our values and keeping our eyes on the goal, we will throw our whole selves into running at the appropriate times and slowing down when we need a different pace.

And we will make it, whole and complete.

# Notes

1. *The Drama of the Gifted Child: The Search for the True Self* (New York: Basic Books, 1982); *Thou Shalt Not Be Aware: Society's Betrayal of the Child* (New York: Meridian Books, New American Library, 1986); *Banished Knowledge: Facing Childhood Injuries* (New York: Doubleday, 1991).
2. Copyright © 1998. The New York Times Company. Reprinted by permission.
3. The American Association of Retired Persons, which recently changed its name to just the letters AARP.
4. For the effects of change, see William Bridges's book *Transitions* (New York: Addison-Wesley, 1989).
5. 1999/2000 Time Inc. New Media. All rights reserved. Reproduction in whole or in part without permission is prohibited. PathFinder is a registered trademark of Time Inc. New Media. Reprinted by permission.
6. L. Powell, A. Roth, and K. Gelburg, "Measurement of Coping Styles Among the Elderly," *Proceedings of the 1987 Public Health Conference on Records and Statistics*, pp. 136–139 (Hyattsville, Md.: U.S. Department of Health and Human Services, 1987). See also R. L. Simons and G. E. West, "Life Changes, Coping Resources, and Health Among the Elderly," *International Journal of Aging and Human Development* 20 (3): 173–189 (1984–1985).
7. Naomi Ridley. Reprinted with permission.
8. One in ten of those over sixty-five have Alzheimer's, while nearly half

of those eighty-five and older are afflicted by it. *Alzheimer's Disease Statistics Fact Sheet,* Alzheimer's Association, 1996.

9. Sue Silvermarie, MSW, *Tales from My Teachers on the Alzheimer's Unit* (Milwaukee, Wis.: Families International, 1996).

10. Naomi Feil, ACSW, *Validation: The Feil Method; How to Help Disoriented Old-Old* (Cleveland: Edward Feil Productions, 1988).

11. *The Summer Day; House of Light.* Copyright © 1990 by Mary Oliver. Reprinted by permission of Beacon Press. (Boston: Beacon Press, 1990), p. 94.

12. When I wrote this page my friend sadly admitted it hit the target. The good news is that he has since quit his job, is moving to a smaller home, and is looking forward to living less dependent on titles or "things." His sense of humor is reviving, and there is new energy in his voice.

13. Mrs. Evelyn Haines. Reprinted with permission.

14. Lucie May Loughborough. Reprinted with permission.

15. My HMO is Kaiser Permanente. I've been a member for over twenty-five years, watching them improve services, asserting myself when it was necessary, and sticking with doctors who care about my health. Knowing that no system is perfect and that even the best medical systems sometimes make serious mistakes, I have to say that, overall, my experience with this organization has been very positive.

16. Jennie Keith, "Global Aging—The View Across Cultures," *Aging Today,* March/April 1996, p. 8.

17. From "The Dance," written by Tony Arrata. Reprinted with permission.

18. Reprinted with permission.

19. Eda LeShan, *It's Better to Be Over the Hill Than Under It: Thoughts on Life After Sixty* (New York: Newmarket Press, 1990), p. 114.

20. Elie Wiesel, *All Rivers Run to the Sea: Memoirs* (New York: Alfred A. Knopf, 1996).

# Bibliography

Albom, Mitch. *Tuesdays with Morrie: An Old Man, A Young Man, and Life's Greatest Lesson.* New York: Doubleday, 1997.

Alexander, Jo, Debi Berrow, Lisa Domitrovich, Margarita Donnelly, and Cheryl McLean, editors. *Women and Aging: An Anthology by Women.* Corvallis, Ore.: Calyx Books, 1986.

Allen, Jessie, and Alan Pifer, editors. *Women on the Front Lines: Meeting the Challenge of an Aging America.* Washington, D.C.: Urban Institute Press, 1993.

Bach, Richard. *Running from Safety: An Adventure of the Spirit.* New York: William Morrow, 1994.

Birren, James E., and Linda Feldman. *Where to Go from Here: Discovering Your Life's Wisdom in the Second Half of Your Life.* New York: Simon & Schuster, 1997.

Bridges, William. *Transitions: Strategies for Coping with the Difficult, Painful, and Confusing Times in Your Life.* Addison-Wesley, 1989.

Buber, Martin. *I and Thou.* New York: Scribner, 1958.

Callahan, Daniel. *Setting Limits: Medical Goals in an Aging Society.* New York: Simon & Schuster, 1987.

Capra, Fritjof. *The Tao of Physics: An Exploration of the Parallels Between Modern Physics and Eastern Mysticism.* New York: Bantam, 1984.

Evans, William, Ph.D., and Irwin Rosenberg, M.D. *BioMarkers: The Ten Determinants of Aging You Can Control.* New York: Simon & Schuster, 1991.

Feil, Naomi. *Validation: The Feil Method; How to Help Disoriented Old-Old.* Cleveland: Edward Feil Productions, 1988. (4614 Prospect Ave., Cleveland, OH 44103.)

Gleick, James. *Chaos: Making of a New Science.* New York: Penguin, 1987.

Goleman, Daniel. *Emotional Intelligence.* New York: Bantam Books, 1995.

Hall, Edward T. *The Dance of Life: The Other Dimension of Time.* New York: Doubleday, 1983.

———. *The Silent Language.* New York: Anchor/Doubleday, 1981.

Hillman, James. *The Soul's Code: In Search of Character and Calling.* New York: Random House, 1996.

Hort, Barbara. *Unholy Hungers: Encountering the Psychic Vampire in Ourselves and Others.* Boston: Shambala, 1996.

Houff, William H. *Infinity in Your Hand: A Guide for the Spiritually Curious.* Boston: Skinner House Books, 1994.

Kabat-Zinn, Jon. *Wherever You Go, There You Are.* New York: Hyperion, 1994.

Laird, Carobeth. *Limbo: A Memoir About Life in a Nursing Home by a Survivor.* Novato, Calif.: Chandler & Sharp, 1987.

LeDoux, Joseph. *The Emotional Brain.* New York: Simon & Schuster, 1986.

LeShan, Eda. *It's Better to Be Over the Hill Than Under It: Thoughts on Life Over Sixty.* New York: Newmarket Press, 1990.

Lustbader, Wendy. *Counting on Kindness: The Dilemmas of Dependency.* New York: Free Press/Macmillan, 1991.

Martz, Sandra Haldeman, editor. *Threads of Experience.* Watsonville, Calif.: Papier-Mache Press, 1996.

Miller, Alice. *The Drama of the Gifted Child: The Search for the True Self.* New York: Basic Books, 1982.

———. *Banished Knowledge: Facing Childhood Injuries.* New York: Doubleday, 1991.

———. *Thou Shalt Not Be Aware: Society's Betrayal of the Child.* New York: Meridian Books/New American Library, 1986.

Morgan, Marlo. *Mutant Message Down Under.* New York: HarperCollins, 1994.

Muller, Wayne. *How, Then, Shall We Live? Four Simple Questions That Reveal the Beauty and Meaning of Our Lives.* New York: Bantam, 1996.

Newton, Ellen. *This Bed My Centre.* Melbourne: McPhee Gribble, 1979.

Oliver, Mary. *House of Light.* Boston: Beacon Press, 1990.

———. *New and Selected Poems.* Boston: Beacon Press, 1992.

Orsborn, Carol. *Enough Is Enough: Exploding the Myth of Having It All.* New York: Putnam, 1986.

Scott-Maxwell, Florida. *The Measure of My Days.* New York: Penguin Books, 1979.

Silvermarie, Sue. *Tales from My Teachers on the Alzheimer's Unit.* Milwaukee, Wis.: Families International, 1996. (11700 West Lake Park Dr., Milwaukee, WI 53224.)

Sogyal, Rinpoche. *The Tibetan Book of Living and Dying.* San Francisco: HarperSan Francisco, 1992.

Somé, Malidoma Patrice. *Of Water and the Spirit.* New York: Tarcher/Putnam, 1994.

Thomas, William H. *Life Worth Living: How Someone You Love Can Still Enjoy Life in a Nursing Home; The Eden Alternative in Action.* Acton, Mass.: VanderWyk & Burnham, 1996.

Upledger, John. *Somato-Emotional Release and Beyond.* Palm Beach Gardens, Fla.: UI Publishing, 1990.

Wiesel, Elie. *All Rivers Run to the Sea: Memoirs.* New York: Alfred A. Knopf, 1996.

Zukav, Gary. *The Dancing Wu Li Masters: An Overview of the New Physics.* New York: Bantam, 1979.

# Acknowledgments

I stood among the ceiling-high stacks at Powell's bookstore several years ago and heaved a sigh of relief. "Thank God," I thought. "There are already so many books, there's certainly no need for me to write one." Relieved, I put my thoughts of writing a book behind me.

A few years later, however, when I needed to spend a week out of town, I found myself at a writers' workshop not too far from home. I went with confidence—published articles in hand—and came home depressed by the rock-bottom certainty that I was really not a writer.

The only problem was that for three or four years a knowledge had been growing inside me—a knowledge that we need to approach our own aging and death in a new way—and it was becoming increasingly hard to keep the knowledge to myself. I gave lectures on it, did seminars on it, even preached about it. Then, three months after the writers' workshop, Don Clarkson (who has yet to write a book) told me that I had to write this book. "It's not a choice, it's an obligation," he said flatly. I groaned, whimpered, protested, and swore. He was relentless. And this book is the result.

Every one of you whom I call "friend" had a part in this. You may not know it, but every good thought, every expression of affection and hospitality, especially the moments of pure silliness, were the fuel that kept me on the straight path from my bed to the computer every morning. Irene and Murray Mehlhoff made their ranch a second home to me, providing all of the above plus good home cooking and large-pet therapy. Jean and Dale Eggers took me in when I was sicker than a dog; Laura Maez constantly amazes me with her facile mind, strength of character, and humor worthy of five good women! Kathleen Worley, I cherish our friendship and am deeply grateful for your help in creating the drama/dialogue group that has now spread across the nation; Louise Dunn, your no-nonsense mind can always set me back on course; and Nevton, I suspect you have as many questions as I do. Keith Melton, my ex-husband, divorced now twenty-one years: after the acrimony we remembered that we really like each other and probably should have forgone the husband-and-wife part. For all the pain and disappointment that accompanied our ten-year marriage, you probably did more to get me here than anyone else. Never questioning my integrity, abilities, or intent, you believed in me. No wonder I love you and still consider you family! My good friend Susan Payton encouraged me every step of the way, giving me her editing skills and reminding me over and over that by the time I finished this book I'd know how to write one. Martha Newell, Joe Coglianese, Nancy Emery, and Carole Warner also read parts of the manuscript and gave needed feedback. Arthur Buck, your outrageousness kept me from taking myself too seriously. Sisters Arnadene Bean and Clare Murphy, you savvy, gorgeous women, you make lunch at the convent a real party! My colleagues at Willamette View, Virginia Gaines, Karen Stahlecker, Kim Buccholz, and CEO Jim Edwards—who had the good sense to hire me—we had so much fun, even (or especially) when things got crazy! Jack and Phyllis Courtney, you gave me family and home in the most literal sense. You hold a permanent and special place in my heart. Sam Eggers, you still haven't found me an eligible llama rancher, but you make up for that with your great sense of humor and fine mind. My early mentors, Parson Frank Evans, the Reverend Walt Johnson, and the Reverend Dr. William Houff, saw something in me worth nurturing. You each modeled an intelligence of heart and mind that deeply influenced my own style of ministry. Mary Goodwin, you're the best champion anyone could have in her corner, and Vickie Schmall, gerontologist extraordinaire, you always manage to see the good. Jean Wilson, Duane Dahlum, Rick Marinelli, Rory Green, Maya Brand, Carole Warner, Tammy Staudt, Sue Jones, Nancy Emery, and Jeanne Gilkeson, professionals all, you became caring companions in my own quest for wholeness and health. Your skill and willingness to go the extra mile enabled me to climb my own mountains. Where would I be without each of you? The Reverend Penny Matthews and the Reverend Trish Knorpp provide me with relaxation and hilarity in Seattle! Barbara Lear, I love your great sense of humor and the huge dictionary I've about worn out; my beautiful friend Ruth Potter, you told me your truth and taught me so much; Dick Lawson, thanks for scintillating conversations that you thought I was able to keep up with; Norma Newhouse—this is in place of writing your name on bathroom walls—I love you. Happy eighty-fifth birthday! Brian Moher, thanks for helping me out with research at the Oregon Geriatric Education Center; Dee Johnson of the Oregon Alzheimer Association, thanks for answering my questions; Carla Rathbun of the Alzheimer Research Alliance, you have an uncanny ability to pull things together! Rebecca Stefoff, thanks for your insight into the mysterious world of publishing. Holly Near, Chris Williamson, and Margie Adams, thank you for singing me into existence.

Judith Riven, my agent, your commitment to this book made it more possible than I'd ever dreamed! To my editor Maria Guarnaschelli, thanks for believing in this project and supporting it with brilliant feedback and much-needed morale boosts!

And finally, to the residents of the Willamette View retirement community: my heart is filled with gratitude for all you gave me to feel and think about. Thank you for trusting me with your struggles and triumphs, your patience, knowledge, and good humor. The world would be a poorer place if you were not in it. You are always in my heart and often on my mind.

# Index

Wiesel, Elie, 201
Wiggins, Brandi, 92
wills, 124
Wink, Walter, 163
wisdom, 37, 145

Witness for Peace, 91
workaholism, 64, 144

Yugoslavia, ethnic hatred in,
88